KU-297-809

THE HOUSEHOLD GUIDE

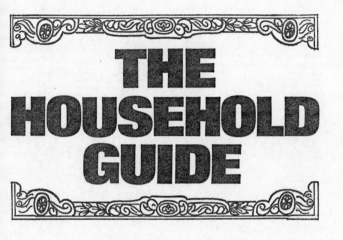

THE HOUSEHOLD GUIDE

ODHAMS BOOKS
LONDON · NEW YORK · SYDNEY · TORONTO

First Published 1967
1st Reprint 1968
2nd Reprint 1969

© J. John Masters & Co. Ltd., 1967
Published for Odhams Books by
THE HAMLYN PUBLISHING GROUP LTD.
LONDON · NEW YORK · SYDNEY · TORONTO
Hamlyn House, Feltham, Middlesex, England
Printed in Great Britain

Contents

Putting things right in the home can be an expensive business, and more often than not the greater part of the cost of household repairs and replacements is in the charge for labour. But there are many jobs that the average householder is capable of tackling successfully without special skills: all that is needed is a little guidance and a few pointers to the right methods and materials.

This Household Guide has been specially compiled by a team of writers who are experts in every aspect of home maintenance and decoration, as well as entertaining in the home. A glance at the list of contents will show the range of subjects dealt with, and to enable the reader to check a particular item quickly there is a comprehensive index on pages 187–192. The book is packed with information on a mass of different subjects and the publishers are confident that it will quickly become an indispensable reference book for the handyman.

Home Maintenance

Sticking doors: A door that has to be slammed and pushed really hard before it will fit into its opening properly can be very irritating. The cause of this can be one of a number of small, easily rectified, faults. First look at the hinges to see if they stay firmly in place when the door moves. If not, take a screwdriver and tighten each of their screws in turn. Some screws may not tighten because the hole has become enlarged. Try a new screw $\frac{1}{4}$ in. or so longer in its place. Or push a small piece of wood – part of an old match will do – into the hole and then try the original screw again.

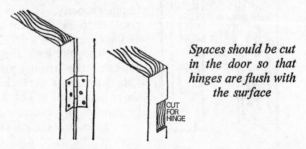

Spaces should be cut in the door so that hinges are flush with the surface

CUT FOR HINGE

Hinges should be rebated into the door and door-frame – i.e. they should be placed in a hole specially cut to receive them so that they are flush with the surrounding timber. If door hinges are not fitted properly in the first place, the door will not close as it should. Unscrew the hinge from its position, first marking round it with a pencil or knife if no hole at all has been cut. Then cut out the hole with a ½-in. firmer chisel and mallet. The method is to cut a groove all round the hole first with a chisel, then chop out the waste. Care must be taken, of course, not to take too much out, but if this happens, pack under the hinge with pieces of card.

A door has to be hung clear of the floor so that it will open and shut properly, therefore it cannot be rested on the floor while the screws are driven home. The best method is to push pieces of card underneath it until it is at just the right height, and get a helper to hold it steady.

Of course, the trouble may not be at the hinges, but at the other side. Look first at the striking plate – the metal plate that contains the cavities for the lock and catch. Like the hinges, this may not have been rebated properly, and, once again, a hole of the right depth will have to be cut with a chisel.

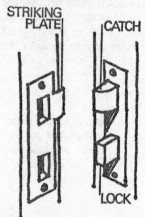

STRIKING PLATE CATCH LOCK

The striking plate must be fitted so that its holes are exactly opposite the catch and lock

Now inspect the catch and lock. If one of these is excessively bright in one spot, it means that it is catching the sides of the hole, and not fitting properly. It may be possible to remove enough of the excess with a flat file from either the lock and/or catch, or the striking plate. Otherwise either the lock or the striking plate will have to be moved up or down the door or frame. If the lock is fitted to the surface of the door, it will probably be easiest to move this. But if it is fitted inside the door, the plate will have to be moved.

8

Sometimes a door will not close properly because it is off square. Look at the door or frame: if a patch of paint is missing, this is a good indication that the door is binding. Make the following test. Close the door, and push a thin piece of card between it and the frame. Move the card all round the door, and where it will not pass, it can be established that the door is sticking. It is possible that by rubbing a bit of candle wax, or wax polish, on the edge of the door, the fault will be cured. Otherwise, it will be necessary to remove a bit of surplus timber with a plane or shaping tool.

Mending a broken window: Window glazing is not a difficult job. First of all, it is necessary to make sure that the frame is prepared properly. Get rid of any jagged edges of glass left in the frame. Do not do this with the hands; use a pair of pincers instead. And, in any case, wear a pair of old gloves. Now get rid of all the old putty in the frame. The professional uses a putty knife to do this, but a handyman can use an old wood chisel and hammer. If

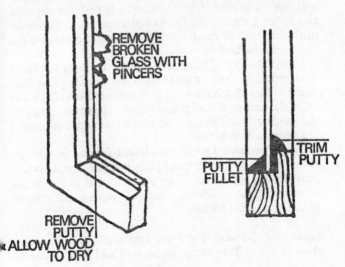

there are any old glazing pins in the frame, do not drive them home into the wood; pull them out with a pair of pincers. Finally, clean up the frame with glasspaper.

The frame should be perfectly dry before carrying on with the rest of the process, so give it a few hours, or even a day, to dry out properly. Protection in the meantime from the weather can be obtained by pinning on a sheet of hardboard or cardboard. When the frame has completely dried out, apply a coat of primer to the whole rebate, and let this dry out, too.

Work the putty in the palms of the hands until it is pliable, and roll it into "worms" $\frac{3}{4}$ in. diameter, and 6 to 9 in. long. Place the "worms" in position in the rebate, and press them home properly with the thumb.

The glass should be ordered so that it is $\frac{1}{16}$ in. all round less than the opening. Place it in position and gently press all round the edges of it with the palms of the hands. As this is done excess putty oozes out, so there should be no air pockets left, and a perfect seal is obtained.

Two glazing pins are needed on each side of the glass, and these should be tapped home gently with the opposite end to the normal striking head of a hammer. This is an operation that obviously needs great care, otherwise the glass may be broken.

Now take more "worms" of putty to form the front fillet, pressing them in place with the thumb. The final shape of this fillet is made by drawing the chisel along it at an angle, cutting out all excess putty. The excess putty on the inside of the frame should also be trimmed off. Paint the putty within a week.

The procedure for metal window-frames is similar, except that a different type of putty is used. Suppliers will provide the right kind if they are told it is for metal window-frames. Glazing pins, of course, cannot be nailed into metal frames.

Loose door-frames: There are two methods of fixing a door-frame in its opening. Either it is held by wall ties let into the mortar while the house is being built, or it is nailed into wooden plugs, which again are fixed into the mortar. It is the door-frames that are nailed to wall-plugs that normally become loose.

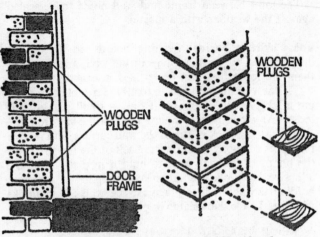

Door-frames are nailed to wall-plugs fitted in between courses of brickwork

The wooden plugs are usually fitted at intervals of four courses, and if the mortar is raked out they can be seen. If there are any nails still holding the frame into plugs, prise them out, and push the frame either backwards or forwards, making sure it is held in position by driving small wooden wedges between it and the wall. There is no point in renewing any of the plugs that are in perfect condition, but defective ones should be replaced by pieces of timber about $3 \times 2 \times \frac{1}{2}$ in., and slightly wedge-shaped. Drive the plugs in as firmly as possible, and saw them off flush with the wall. At this stage, too, carry out any necessary repointing – use small bags of mortar ready mixed. Water of course, has to be added.

Now bring the frame into position, using a length of string with a weight on it as a plumb-line and bob, to make sure the frame is exactly vertical – it is imperative that it should be so. Fix it to the plugs with oval-headed nails driven below the surface and the resulting holes filled.

The joint between frame and wall needs to be sealed against the weather with a mastic.

Loose skirting boards: Skirting boards are fixed, like door-frames, to wooden plugs in the wall, and if any of them are loose they can be re-fixed in exactly the same way. But it seems a pity to go to all the trouble of removing a long length of board, if only a small part of it is loose. An alternative is to ease the board away from the wall, clean the back of it and the wall surface, and place a few spots of epoxy resin on the back of the board. Press the board to the wall and, to hold it in place while the adhesive sets, place some heavy weights in position, holding the board firmly against the wall (clean bricks will do). Leave the weights in place for at least 12 hours.

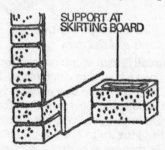

SUPPORT AT SKIRTING BOARD

Loose skirting boards can be secured by using an adhesive

Loose floorboards: If the floorboards in a house start to creak, the reason could be that they have worked loose – i.e. the nails are no longer holding them securely to the joists. Walk round the room carefully finding out where the trouble spots are, and pull out the nails with a claw hammer or pair of pincers. Stand on the boards and press them down in their correct position, and fix them securely again, starting from the middle board, or group of boards if there is more than one, and working outwards. The fixing can be done with either slightly stouter and longer nails, punched below the surface, or (a better, but more tedious and expensive process) with screws, countersunk so that their heads are below the surface.

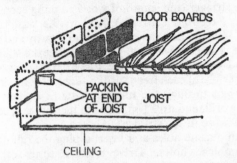

Replace packing around joists to cure a springing floor

Springing floor: When a floor moves up and down as it is walked on, it is said to be a springing floor. This is a trouble often found in older houses where central heating has recently been installed. It could well be that the floorboards have warped, and in this case treatment as for loose floorboards might effect a cure, although the boards could be so badly warped that they have to be replaced.

On the other hand, it could be the joist at fault. The end of a floor joist is inserted into a hole in a load-bearing wall, and sometimes it may be necessary to insert packing in the cavity to make the joist a better fit. If this packing, for any reason, falls out, the joist will work loose.

To tackle this job is by no means easy for, except in the case of a ground floor where there is easy access underneath by means of a cellar, it will be necessary to prise up three floorboards near the wall, and pull away the skirting board. This will probably reveal that the packing has come adrift – in a bedroom it may well be resting on the downstairs ceiling – or it may just be loose. Replace the packing by driving it home firmly with a mallet or hammer. If the packing is in bad condition, replace it with wedge-shaped pieces of wood of an appropriate size. Then replace the boards and skirting.

Loose stringer: It is not uncommon, as a house gets older, for the stringer (the length of wood running each side of the steps of your staircase) fixed to the wall to work loose. It would be a major job to pull it away and refix it, so here is an easy way out, providing that the staircase is in good condition. Near the top of the stringer, level with the nose of each tread, drill a series of $\frac{1}{4}$-in. diameter holes right through the timber. Now fit a masonry bit into the drill, and drill $\frac{1}{4}$-in. holes in the wall as a continuation of those in the stringer.

Clean out the holes and insert a plug the full depth of the combined holes. Drive home a series of No. 8 countersunk screws large enough to pass through the stringer and well into the wall. The holes made by countersinking the screws can be filled with plastic filler.

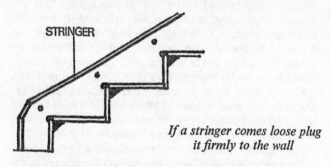

STRINGER

If a stringer comes loose plug it firmly to the wall

Leaking lavatory pipe: A leak in the joint between the lavatory pan outlet and the soil pipe is often found in many homes – you get the tell-tale signs of water on the floorboards. Inspect the joint and, if the cement has come away from the joint, then the fault can be cured by the handyman.

Put a flat tray or bowl under the joint on the floor, and

rake out the mortar with an old wood chisel – do not use a mallet as this may damage the pan. When the cement has been removed, there may still be grit in the joint; and this can be removed with a clean paint-brush.

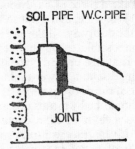

The joint between the lavatory pan outlet and the soil pipe sometimes leaks

The joint is sealed with gaskin or hemp that has had mastic rubbed on to it. Wrap the gaskin round the lavatory pipe, and push it well into the joint with the chisel, until you can test with your fingers that the joint is sound. Complete the joint with mastic or a mortar of one part cement to one part sand. There are gases in a foul drain, and so this job should be finished as quickly as possible. Work with the door and window open.

Leaking leaded lights: If water seeps through your leaded lights, mark the position of the leaks with a piece of chalk during a downpour of rain. The joint between horizontal and vertical strips of lead is usually spot-soldered and you must be careful not to break it. But with a penknife blade you should be able to ease the lead strip away from the glass, but taking great care lest you stretch the lead. Use the blade to clean out dirt and old filling, and make sure the cavity is dry.

Take some mastic, roll it into "worms" about $\frac{1}{16}$ in. in diameter, place the mastic in the cavity, and use the knife blade to spread it out evenly. Press the top of the lead against the pane, so that the mastic is forced out, and trim it off with a knife.

15

Water-sealing an outside door: A door can fit so badly in its opening that rainwater is driven under the bottom of it in large quantities, especially if the door is badly exposed to driving winds. Here is the cure. First measure the gap at the bottom of the door. Take a piece of hardwood of the same thickness and, say, $1\frac{1}{2}$ in. wide, and cut it so that its length equals the width of the doorway. If the gap is of such dimensions that it is impossible to buy timber of equal thickness, then buy the next size up and plane it, or reduce it to size with a sanding disc in a power tool. Fix the timber in place at the foot of the door opening. If the floor is of timber, the fixing should be by means of screws and waterproof adhesive. On a floor of solid concrete, the screws will have to be driven into wall-plugs (see page 21). Now take a length of $6 \times \frac{1}{2}$-in. timber and fix it to the bottom of the door, using panel pins and water-proof adhesive, to seal the gap effectively.

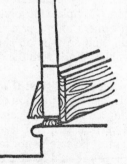

Sealing an outside door to prevent rainwater driving in beneath it

Broken floorboards: When a floorboard is damaged along all, or most, of its length, then it is better to take the whole board up and renew it entirely. When, however, part of it is damaged, it is necessary to replace only a small section.

The damaged section has to be cut out up to the edges of the nearest joist. The nails in the floorboards will show where the joists are, and carpenters aim to put these nails

A small section of broken floorboard can be replaced

right in the middle. A normal width for a joist is 2 in. From these facts it is possible to calculate the approximate position of the edge. Make a test boring with a drill about $\frac{1}{2}$ in. farther away from the joist than you had calculated, and with the drill, or perhaps a small chisel or bradawl, locate the exact position. Now make a series of drill borings for the whole width of the floorboard, right at the edge of the joist. With a thin padsaw join up these holes, or chop through to them with a chisel and mallet. Repeat the process at the other end, and you will be able to pull the damaged board away. If, however, the floor is a tongued and grooved one of such recent construction that no appreciable shrinkage has yet taken place, the tongues and grooves may be such a tight fit that it is difficult, or even impossible, to take the board up. In this case, it is necessary to chop off the tongues. Place a chisel on the gap between the boards and strike it with a mallet, moving along as each section is completed. It may be necessary to do this on one side only, or on both.

Short lengths of 2×1-in. timber should now be screwed to the sides of the joists, and it might be an additional precaution to smear a little glue on the meeting surfaces. A new length of board should now be bought and nailed to these pieces of timber. Do not buy a tongued and grooved board, even if the rest of the floor is tongued and grooved, if it appears that there will be any difficulty about inserting it in place correctly. On a very old floor, where a lot of shrinkage has taken place it may be necessary to use a board with a tongue to cover the gap effectively. It must be emphasized that this method is satisfactory only for short pieces of isolated board. Where a floor is extensively damaged it must, for safety's sake, be renewed quickly and completely by an expert.

Worn steps: It is possible to repair steps that have worn down with the action of the weather, or years of footsteps passing over them. Colour additives can also be bought for concrete, so it is possible to change the colour of the step whilst the repair is being carried out.

The surface of the step should be cleaned and roughened up, and 1-in. thick board placed all round it, and held in place by bricks. If possible the boards should be 1 in. away from the step, and a 1-in. layer of concrete should be placed on top of the step during the repair. If this is not possible for any reason, a bonding additive should be bought from a builders' merchant, and added to the concrete mix given below. Small granite chippings can be placed at the bottom of the timber framework at strategic places to keep the boards away from the step.

The concrete should consist of 1 part cement, $1\frac{1}{2}$ parts sand and 3 parts small chippings or shingle. It may be possible to buy locally small quantities of sand and cement already mixed to those proportions. The concrete should first of all be mixed dry, then the water added. Most amateurs make the mistake of adding too much water; there should be just enough to make the mix workable, but not so much that it is sloppy and slumps all over the place.

Now thoroughly damp the step, and start to apply the concrete. First it should be pushed down between the step and board, and it needs to be rammed down and compacted very firmly, to make sure no pockets of air are left. When the front and sides have been filled, the top of the step can be covered, again, making sure that the concrete has been well rammed down. Use a steel float or a trowel to smooth off the top of the step, but do not overwork the concrete by stroking it too much. During this process make sure that there is a slight slope from back to front of the step, so that rainwater will drain away and not lodge in place.

Cover the step with thick paper to protect the concrete, and take precautions to stop anyone from standing on the step. The form these precautions must take will depend on the step's location. In a busy traffic area, it might be necessary to place a board over it on which people can walk. At the top end of the garden, which is hardly ever visited, perhaps just some string tied to stakes, in the manner for stopping birds from alighting on a newly-sown lawn, would do.

Strip away the timber the following day, and inspect the front and sides for any air pockets that may have formed due to the compacting not having been thorough enough. If there are any, they should be filled by a mix of 1 part cement to 2 parts clean sand.

The protective material should then be put back in place and left there for at least four days, but a week if possible, to allow the concrete to harden properly before the step has to be used.

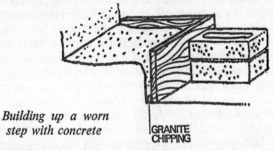

Building up a worn step with concrete

GRANITE CHIPPING

Fixing curtain track: Curtain fittings normally consist of a length of track with brackets to hold the track in place. Parts are usually supplied separately. The method for fixing the brackets to the track varies with different makes of fitting, and the manufacturer's instructions should be closely read and followed. Here, however, are some tips on fixing the brackets to the wall or window-frame.

The first decision must be about the length of the curtains. If they are to be of short length, inside the

19

window opening, the fixing problems are relatively simple: brackets are merely screwed into wood. It sometimes happens, however, that where thick curtains are used, or curtains with a good lining, then these brackets do not hold the track sufficiently far away from the window-frame, and as the curtains are opened and closed they rub against the timber, making it difficult to operate them, and causing them to wear out sooner than they otherwise would.

There are two ways of overcoming this. It is possible to make a set of what might be termed washers from a spare, small piece of hardboard or plywood, and the washers can be placed on the screw, but between the bracket and window-frame, thus keeping them farther apart. The other way is to tack a narrow piece of thin lath or battening on to the window-frame, painting it the same colour as the frame so that it is unobtrusive, and then screwing the track brackets to this.

If full-length curtains are desired, the fixing has to be outside the opening and on top of it, and it is here that a problem arises. For underneath the plaster will be found not brickwork, which it is fairly easy to drill so that wall-plugs can be fitted, but a concrete lintel, and this is much tougher, especially where it is preferred to bore the holes with a drill, rather than a jumping tool and hammer.

Concrete consists of cement, sand, and flint aggregate. The drill will cut easily through cement and sand, but when it meets the flint, it will either come to a full stop, or be deflected from its proper path. A method that many professionals use is to start the hole with a drill – either hand or electric – withdraw the drill when they meet trouble, and strike a few blows with a hammer and jumping tool, to remove the flint, then continuing with the drill.

A better fixing is obtained if the brackets are not screwed directly to the wall-plugs, but if first of all a length of battening, say $1\frac{1}{2} \times \frac{1}{2}$ in., is fixed to the wall, and the brackets are screwed to this.

Another popular length for curtains, although much more expensive in the amount of fabric it uses, is to fix the track to the ceiling. Care must be taken in doing this, and it must be remembered that the longer the curtain, the heavier the weight of the fabric, and this can mount up to quite considerable proportions, requiring a really firm fixing to hold securely and firmly in place for a long time. Once again it is better to fix a length of battening in place first, and screw the track brackets to this.

A ceiling consists of a very thin layer of plaster, or plaster board, fixed to joists. A screw driven into the plaster will not hold the weight of the curtains – indeed it would hold very little weight at all. It is, therefore, essential that the screws should go into the joists.

How to find the joists? Look in the room above, and the position of the floorboard nails will show where the joists are. If there is no room above, but merely a loft, you can actually see the joists. Measure their distance in relation to a convenient wall, and their distance apart which will be the same in each case, and transfer these readings to the room below. If there is no access above the room, it is sometimes possible to find the joists by tapping the ceiling lightly with the knuckles, or a piece of wood. A tap between the joists should give off a hollow sound; a tap right on them will sound more solid. If desired, a test boring with a drill can be carried out, because this hole will subsequently be covered up. If inspection reveals no joist in a convenient position for fixing the track, then the aid of an expert should be enlisted, or the plan for ceiling-to-floor curtains abandoned.

Screwing into a wall: There are two main ways of making a fixing into a wall. The first is to use a wall-plug, and the second a plugging compound.

First the wall-plug method. A system of numbering is used to indicate the thickness of screws. The screws the amateur will most commonly come across in jobs around the house are Nos. 6, 8 and 10, although he may find smaller and bigger ones on his car or on the domestic electrical equipment. This numbering is carried throughout the whole wall-fixing terminology. Thus wall-plugs are sold to fit a certain size of screw, and boring equipment is described as fitting a certain size of wall-plug.

The first step is to determine the size of screw. For general work around the home, such as screwing battens to a wall, No. 8 is a convenient size, but other sizes may be encountered if an item such as a towel-rail comes complete with fixing screws. Next its length must be decided. In deciding this, it must be remembered that the screw should go at least $\frac{1}{2}$ in. into the actual masonry (not counting the plaster facing) for even a light fixture, but go in 1 in. – even farther in some cases – for heavier fixings. Thus if a 1-in. thick batten is to be screwed to a wall to hold, perhaps, a book shelf, a screw of 2 in. or better still $2\frac{1}{2}$ in. in length is needed.

Next, wall-plugs to fit the diameter and length of the screw should be ordered. Wall-plugs that are too long can easily be cut with a blow from a chisel, or with a sharp knife. Finally, a masonry bit, to fit a hand-operated or electric drill, or a jumping tool of the correct diameter, should be used to make a hole in the right place, and of the right depth. Test the depth of the hole from time to time by withdrawing the boring tool, removing the spoil, and inserting the plug. When the hole is complete, the wall-plug is pushed home, and the screw can then be driven into it.

A plugging compound is a powdery, fibrous material that binds together when water is added. It is rolled between the palms of the hands into a long, cylindrical shape, and it can then be pushed into a hole that has been bored to receive it. A small metal tool is usually given with packets of plugging compound, so that it can be rammed home properly, and a starting hole for the screw made in it.

The point about a plugging compound is that it is not

necessary to bore an accurate hole. Just so long as it is not too short and not too thin, it will do. There is no question of its being too long or too thick, since the plugging compound can adapt itself to any size or shape. Then the screw can be driven in, to give a very firm fixing.

When a series of separate metal objects – such as coat hooks, shelf brackets, curtain-rail brackets, kitchen utensil hooks, etc. – has to be fixed to a wall, it is not good practice to fix them direct. A better method is to screw a length of wood to the wall first, and then fix the metal objects to this. This involves fewer fixing points to the wall, for whereas there will be two or three screw holes in a coat hook, the timber need be screwed to the wall only every 12 or 18 in. A firmer, more positive fixing can be obtained by screwing the length of timber to the wall, than with individual hooks. There will be less damage to be made good to the plaster, should it ever be necessary to remove the fixing, and the resultant effect can look neater. In the case of the coat hooks already mentioned, these could be mounted in full view in the hall on a length of good-looking, attractively polished hardwood.

Screwing into timber: Many amateurs make the mistake of thinking there is nothing to learn about this job. They discover their mistake when they try to drive a thick screw into hard timber, and find that it will not go in. In fact, there is a proper procedure for this job. With a very tiny screw that is to go into very soft wood, then the screw can be driven home with no preliminary preparation. Otherwise, holes have to be bored to receive the various parts of the screw.

A screw can be divided into three parts. First comes the head. This can be countersunk (the type meant for driving flush with the surface); roundhead (a head that will stand proud of the work) which is used mainly for fixing metal, such as shelf brackets, to wood; and raised head, which is a compromise between these two, and is

23

used often for higher-class ironmongery, such as fixing door handles in place.

Immediately below the head comes the shank, and after that the thread, which tapers off to a fine point.

Holes have to be bored to receive these various parts. First should be drilled the pilot hole, which the thread needs. This hole should be as long as the screw, although no harm is done if it is longer. Next drill the clearance hole for the shank. Try to keep this to exactly the same depth as the shank. Finally, a countersunk hole has to be drilled with a special bit to receive a countersunk head that is being driven into hard wood. No hole is needed for the other types of head, or for countersunk heads in very soft wood. The table below gives the sizes of clearance and pilot hole needed for various sizes of screw.

Screw size	6	8	10	12	14	16	18
Clearance	$\frac{1}{8}$ in.	$\frac{5}{32}$ in.	$\frac{3}{16}$ in.	$\frac{7}{32}$ in.	$\frac{1}{4}$ in.	$\frac{9}{32}$ in.	$\frac{5}{16}$ in.
Pilot hole	$\frac{5}{64}$ in.	$\frac{3}{32}$ in.	$\frac{1}{8}$ in.	$\frac{1}{8}$ in.	$\frac{5}{32}$ in.	$\frac{3}{16}$ in.	$\frac{3}{16}$ in.

If a drill bit to the exact size of hole above is not available, choose one slightly smaller if possible, to give the screw a good push fit.

Types of nail: Panel pin – From $\frac{3}{8}$ in. to $1\frac{1}{2}$ in. in length. Used for all fine work, and for such jobs as pinning building boards and plywood, and fixing mouldings.

Hardboard nail – Usually $\frac{3}{4}$ in. Specially designed for fixing hardboard. When driven in, the head is lost below the surface. Usually plated with a non-rusting material.

Round-wire nail – Used for all types of carpentry. Obtainable with a galvanized finish for fixing the various building boards.

Oval brad – Better than the round-wire nail for good class carpentry.

Floor nail – For fixing floorboards to joists, although oval brads are often used for this work. The square point

24

of this nail cuts the wood fibres without splitting the timber.

Clout nail – For nailing felts etc. to a roof. Usually has a galvanized finish. In various sizes from ½ to 2 in.

Corrugated fastener – From ⅜ to 1 in. For joining boards edge to edge, and for joining framework that will later be covered with hardboard or plywood.

Using a hammer: Always wipe a hammer face clean before you start a job. The face picks up grease and dirt from the nail heads, and will then not drive true, particularly on fine work. The nearer to the end of the hammer that you hold your handle, the less effort will be demanded.

Withdrawing nails: When withdrawing a nail with a claw hammer or pair of pincers, place a piece of thin wood or plywood on the face of the work, and lever on this, to avoid bruising. If the work is damaged slightly, the dent can often be raised if it is liberally doused in water, preferably boiling, then rubbed down with glasspaper.

Fixing bookshelves: The alcoves on each side of the chimney breast are an ideal place for fixing bookshelves, because you can use three walls for support, and this area would otherwise probably be so much wasted space. Wherever the shelves are fitted, however, the following principles should be observed.

Books are heavy objects, and impose quite a strain on timber. This timber, too, has to face up to the strain of alternate extremes of hot and cold during the winter months. Stout timber should, therefore, always be used. Many public libraries use 1-in. thick timber. This might look too cumbersome in a small home, and would be expensive. So ¾-in. thick timber could be used as a compromise. Certainly, ½-in. timber is too fragile.

The shelves should be supported on battens at each end, and along their back. Timber something like 2 × 1 in. or 1½ × ¾ in. should be used, or a more decorative moulding – provided it is ¾ or 1 in. thick – can take its place. This type of bearer would look better if it were mitred at the corners.

It is not advisable to have a span of more than 3 ft. without some intermediate support. This support would be a length of the same timber as the shelves nailed through from the top and bottom. If a whole series of intermediate supports are to be placed one above the other, this type of fixing would be impossible, and the support can be held in place with thin fillets of wood nailed to the shelves. If records are to be kept on the shelves, a safer maximum spacing would be 18 in.

The spacing of the shelves should be decided on to take account of the sizes of book that are to be stored. As a design point, it is usual to have the bigger books on the bottom shelf. Sizes of books vary, but here is a rough guide. Paperbacks are about 7 in. tall and $4\frac{1}{2}$ in. wide; hardback novels are often something like 8 in. tall and $5\frac{1}{2}$ in. wide; art and other heavily illustrated books are often 13×11 in.

Door bells: First decide whether a bell, chimes or buzzer is the preferred noise. The order of these appliances according to volume of noise they make, starting with the loudest, is bell, chimes, buzzer. Therefore, for a large home and family, a bell, or at least chimes, would be preferred. The order according to price, starting with the cheapest, is usually buzzer, bell, chimes.

The double "ding-dong" of the usual chimes gets lost against the noise of television or radio, and might not be heard by older people who may be slightly deaf. Chimes with a longer series of notes are available, although they are more expensive.

In a home that has many callers at the back door it might be as well to have some kind of warning instrument there. Obviously, this should be different from that at the front door, and a combination of bell and buzzer, or chimes and buzzer, should be considered. It is also possible to have two bells, each with its own distinctive note. More convenient still are the chimes that can be connected to pushes at two different doors, yet give a different note according to which push is pressed.

Conversely, it is also possible to have two warning instruments connected to the same push – there could be one in a living-room, and another in a kitchen; or one upstairs and one downstairs. In some cases, it is possible to flick a switch to make only one of these operational at a time. Thus a family going to bed could cut out the downstairs bell, and have only that upstairs working.

A wide range of bell-pushes is available. Illuminated pushes help the caller after dark, and they help the householder to find the keyhole when he is returning home late at night. These, however, will work only on mains operated systems, and not battery operated ones.

Next, it must be decided whether the system is to be mains or battery operated, and this is a decision that must be taken before any equipment is bought, because some instruments can only be worked by one or the other. A mains system is the dearest to buy and install, because a transformer is necessary. It will, however, be cheaper to run, but only marginally so, because a battery can be expected to last from six to twelve months.

A mains system needs to be installed by someone with a knowledge of electricity, so the householder who wants to fit everything himself should think in terms of a battery system. Battery systems are often sold as do-it-yourself kits, with a bell or chimes into which the battery is fitted out of sight. Installation is then very simple. Bore a $\frac{1}{4}$-in. hole in the door-frame and pass a length of the twin bell wire through it. Screw the ends of this wire to the terminals of the push, and screw the push to the door-frame. Fix the bell or chimes in the position inside the home that it will occupy, and connect the other ends of the wire to it.

If an instrument without provision for accommodating the battery is used, find a suitable place to hide the battery.

This could be on a ledge high up near the front door, inside a meter cupboard, or in a fanlight. One wire of the twin flex should run to the instrument from the push in the normal way. A length of wire is then needed from push to battery and from warning instrument to battery.

Wherever possible, the wire should be run along wooden door-frames and skirting boards, and be fixed with staples at approximately 9-in. intervals.

First aid for burst pipes: Of course, it is possible to avoid the problem of burst pipes altogether, by insulating all exposed pipes properly, but it is no use giving this advice once the damage has been done. The first job, once it is discovered that water does not emerge when a tap has been turned on, is to shut off all the stopcocks. The wise householder should study his plumbing system long before there is any possibility of trouble. He should know where all the stopcocks in his house are, and know exactly which part of the plumbing they control. In fact, it is not a bad idea to label the stopcocks. The main stopcock will probably be outside the house, just by the garden gate, and it is advisable to sprinkle salt on its cover during cold weather, so that it will be readily accessible during an emergency.

When all the stopcocks are turned off, the job of tracing the trouble can begin. Use the tap as a starting point and work away from it. Plumbers thaw out a pipe by using a blowlamp, but the unskilled amateur should not copy this method. A cloth soaked in warm water or a hair dryer is safer. These warming appliances should be moved along the affected pipe, or pipes, in an attempt to unfreeze them. Eventually the trouble spot will be located. It is possible that, with a little luck, no damage will have been done to the pipe, and the water supply can be turned on and the household continue as normal.

If the pipe has burst, however, a plumber should be called immediately. Since several other households might be in the same position, however, it is likely that there will be a long waiting list. Certain temporary repairs can be effected in the meantime. Plastic metal can be used to block up the hole. If the pipe bulges out, it should first of all be gently tapped back into place with a mallet and a piece of wood. A bandage of adhesive tape can be wrapped tightly round the pipe. If there is a spare piece of hosepipe handy, this can be placed over the slit, and held in place with string or, better still, Jubilee clips. Any one of these repairs – or several of them together – may be so effective that the domestic water supply can be restored. It would be a mistake, however, to think of them as permanent.

Incidentally, many modern homes with copper plumbing think that this is resistant to frost bursts, and that they need not take any precautions. This is not so. It is true that copper has a greater elasticity than either lead or galvanized iron, which are the more traditional plumbing metals, but it can still be pierced as the ice inside it starts to expand.

Cisterns, especially those in outside lavatories, are liable to freeze up in frosty weather. It is a good idea, when frost is forecast, to sprinkle a little salt into them and the lavatory pan before going to bed at night. If they do freeze, they will not burst, or spring a leak. But the action of the ice might bend the arm holding the ball valve. This would allow more water than necessary to enter the cistern, and there might be an overflow. It is therefore prudent to inspect a lavatory cistern in which the water has frozen, and bend back the arm to its proper position if needed.

Using adhesives: Modern glues are so good that, if you use them to stick two items together and then try to pull them apart, more often than not the break will not occur at the glue line. It is also now possible to use them to make repairs when formerly the broken object would have been thrown away, or else expensive welding would have been involved. There are only two conditions that

29

must be observed. You must use a glue only for the purpose for which it was intended and secondly, it is vital that you follow the makers' instructions. The following list shows what sticks what.

Building boards such as hardboard, plywood and block-board: Bostik Pads and Adhesive 1440; Croid Polystik, and Universal; Dunlop LP; Evo-Stik Impact; Britfix 99; Dundex Synthetic Adhesive; Uhu; Clam 3; Rawlbond; Unibond A.G.F.; Tretobond 404.

Carpets: Armstrong LI28; Bostik 1; Copydex; Fabrex; Dunlop A390 and A1020; Evo-Stik Impact; Britfix 99; Dundex Carpet Adhesive; Rawlplug Durofast; Unibond.

Ceramic Floor Tiles: Bostik C; Croid Polystik; Dunlop CT-S; Fortafix Adhesive Tile Cement; Rawlplug Tile Cement; Unibond; Tretobond 737.

Ceramic wall tiles: Bostik Ceramic Tile Adhesive; Araldite; Dunlop CT–W; Fortafix Tile Cement; Britfix 99; Plycol Tilefix; Rawlplug Tile Cement; Cerafix; Fleximent Ceramic Tile Cement; Polyfix.

Cork: Armstrong L128 and L530; Bostik C; Copydex; Croid Universal; Dunlop LP; Evo-Stik 837; Britfix 99; Plycol Cork and Lino Adhesive; Rawlplug Durofast; Unibond; Tretobond 658.

Fireplace tiles: Tiluma Fireplace Tile Cement; Croid Universal; Dunlop CT–S; Fortafix Tile Cement; Britfix 99; Clam 2; Plycol Tilefix; Rawlplug Tile Cement; Unibond Cerafix; Polycell Fireproof Cement.

Glass: Bostik 1; Araldite; Evo-Stik Impact; Fortafix Liquid Porcelain Adhesive; Britfix 66 Balsa Cement; Double Bond Epoxide Adhesive; Uhu; Rawlplug Durofix; Unibond; Tretobond 412.

Hessian: Bostik 1; Croid Polystik; Fabrex; Dunlop A390 and A1020; Evo-Tex SL820; Britfix 99; Dundex Carpet Adhesive; Clam 143; Rawlbond; Unibond; Vinylstik; Polycell Heavy Duty.

Leathercloth: Gloy Multiglue; Bostik 1; Croid 810, Universal and Clear Liquid Glue; Dunlop LP; Evo-Stik

Impact; Britfix 33 Liquid; Dundex Synthetic Adhesive; Clam 2, 7 and 143; Rawlplug Durofast; Unibond; Tretobond 404.

Linoleum: Armstrong L128 and L530; Bostik C; Copydex; Croid Universal; Dunlop LP; Evo-Stik 873; Britfix 99; Plycol Cork and Lino Adhesive; Lignin Paste Adhesive; Rawlplug Durofast; Unibond; Tretobond 658.

Metal: Bostik 7; Araldite; Evo-Stik Impact; Britfix 66 Balsa Cement; Double Bond Epoxide Adhesive; Uhu; Rawlplug Durofast; Tretobond 412.

Polystyrene: Armstrong H602; Tapwata Cold Water Paste Powder; Bostik 4055; Fixuma Wall Tile Adhesive; Copydex Do-It-Yourself; Croid Polystik; Dunlop SF; Evo-Stik 863; Britfix 99; Clam 24 and 143; Plycol 1212; Rawlbond; Unibond or E.P.A.; Tretobond 282; Styrenestik; Vinylstik; Polycell Heavy Duty; Adpep.

Pottery: Bostik 7; Chuk'ka China Cement; Araldite; Evo-Stik Impact; Fortafix Liquid Porcelain Adhesive; Britfix 66 Balsa Cement; Double Bond Epoxide Adhesive; Uhu; Rawlplug Durofix; Unibond.

Rubber: Armstrong L235 and L600; Bostik C; Copydex; Dunlop RF; Evo-Stik 873; Rawlplug Durofast; Tretobond 737.

Vinyl: Armstrong L600, L510, L90 and L235; Bostik 4050; Dunlop PT; Evo-Stik 873; Britfix 99; Plycol Tilefix; Rawlbond; Tretobond 659 and 658; Fleximent Ceramic Tile Cement.

Heavy Wallpapers: Tapwata Cold Water Paste – with added Dextrine; Croid 817; Rawlbond; Unibond Unidextra; Vinylstik; Clam; Polycell H.D.; Lap FP.

Light Wallpapers: Tapwata Cold Water Paste Powder; Octopus Cold Water Paste Powder; Clam Cold Water Paste Powder; Unipaste; Polycell; Lapcell.

Vinyl coated wallpapers: Croid 817; Evo-Stik Wall Veneer Adhesive; Clam 143; Plycol Tilefix (vinyl adhesive); Rawlbond; Unibond; Vinylstik; Polycell Heavy Duty; Lap FP.

Wood: Gloy Multiglue; Bostik Bond PVA; Aerolite 306; Croid Aero, Universal and Clear Liquid Glue; Polystik; Dunlop LP; Evo-Stik Resin W; Britfix 55; Double Bond Epoxide Adhesive; Uhu; Clam 7; Plycol Wood Block Adhesive; Rawlplug Durofast; Unibond; Timbabond 606; Lokfast.

Wood block flooring: Bostik Bond PVA; Croid Aero, Universal and Polystik; Britfix 99; Clam 21; Plycol Parquetry Adhesive; Rawlbond; Unibond.

Erecting a clothes post: It has been calculated that an average line of washing weighs 5 cwt. when it is first put out to dry. In a stiff breeze the strain on the line and the points of anchorage can reach half a ton. We point out these facts merely to show how important it is to get a firm fixing if the newly washed clothes are not to finish up on the ground.

Clothes posts can be either tubular steel or timber, bought from a local hardware shop, or you can make one yourself from timber. If you are buying one, ask the shopkeeper if there is any recommended maximum length of clothes line to be used with the post. If you are making one, a timber such as Columbian pine, which is straight grained and very resilient, with a certain amount of spring, is suitable.

For a 10-ft. line, use timber at least 2 in. sq.; for 15 ft., 3 × 2 in., with the 2 in. side facing the line; for a 20-ft. line 3 in. sq. Before erecting the post, treat it with an exterior timber preservative. Stout 4-in. nails should be driven into each face of the post about 4 in. from the bottom, to act as ties.

How far should the post be sunk into the ground? A good rule is to allow 4 in. for every ft. above the ground. This means that if a post 6 ft. out of the ground is required – and this is a good, average height, although there may be factors calling for one higher or lower – then the total length should be 8 ft., with 2 ft., sunk into the ground.

The post should be sunk in concrete, made up of 1 part of cement, 2 of sand and 3 shingle or chippings. The hole should be dug 6 in. all round oversize. First a 1-in. layer of concrete should be spread on the floor of the hole, a brick placed on this concrete, and the base of the post placed on the brick. While someone holds the post upright, pour the rest of the concrete down into the hole, and make sure it is well compacted and rammed into the hole. Use a plumb line to check that the post is perfectly upright, and leave the concrete to set for seven days before you use the post. The hooks to hold the clothes line should be placed 3 in. down from the top. These can be fixed in place either when the concrete has set, or before you start to put up the pole.

If the hook for the other end of the line is to be fixed to the house wall, rather than to another post, then this, too, needs to be chosen with great care, for it will have to face just as great a strain as the post. An eye type rawlbolt is a suitable fixing. The hole for one of these should be positioned in the centre of a brick, and not in the mortar. It should be made with great care, using either the special rawlplug tool, or masonry bit, used at a very slow speed. Care has to be taken in using rawlbolts, for they can split the brickwork, if you use one too large for the hole. They do, however, offer a very firm fixing.

Another type of fixing, although not so strong, is to use a staple fixed into one of the mortar joints. The safest way is to rake out the mortar to a depth of 2 in., forming a V-shaped cavity with the widest part inside the wall. Place the staple in the hole, and fill it up with a mortar of one part of cement to three of sand, making sure that this is well rammed home.

Wiring up a three-pin plug: The correct colour coding for three-core electrical flex is red for live or positive, black for negative and green for earth. The terminals, inside the plug, are usually marked L for live, N for negative and E for earth. A strong word of warning here. It is not unknown for foreign electrical apparatus to arrive in Britain on which an entirely different colour coding is used. In some instances, the red has been the earth wire, and to connect up an earth wire to a live terminal is extremely dangerous. Anyone buying foreign electrical equipment should always ask his dealer if the usual British colour coding is being followed.

Unblocking a waste pipe: When water runs sluggishly, or not at all, out of a sink, washbasin or bath, first try pushing a length of wire down into the waste pipe to try to dislodge the dirt. If that fails, use a rubber force cup. These cost only a few shillings, and every household should have one. Put the waste plug in position, if the water is running out to a certain extent, and fill the sink to a depth of two inches. Fill up the overflow hole temporarily with old rags. Pull out the waste plug, place the force cup over the hole and start to press down on it so that the pressure is exerted on the column of water in the pipe.

After each downward stroke, try the effect of pulling upwards, which will cause a sucking motion that will also tend to free the dirt. If this does not work, it will be necessary to take out the clearing cap at the bottom of the U-trap in the waste bend, not forgetting to place a bucket underneath first, and dislodge the blockage with wire. Regular use of the force cup, at the slightest sign of any sluggishness in the dispersal of water, will stop any build-up of dirt in the pipes. It is also a good idea to place crystals of household soda in the waste hole, and pour on boiling water to dissolve them, and so carry the solution down into the pipe. This will clean the inside of the pipe, and stop any gathering of solid material. Remember to carry out this maintenance on the bath, as well as the more obvious trouble spot of the kitchen sink, for the waste trap to this is often inaccessible, especially on modern, panelled ones, and you might have to call in a plumber to help.

Baby-proof windows: Here is a very simple method of ensuring that, while the parents will be able to do so, a young child will find it quite impossible to open his bedroom window. On each side of the window, and towards the top, drill a ⅜-in. diameter hole so that it goes right through the fixed and the opening part of the window frame. Fit a length of ⅜-in. dowel cut to a length so that it sticks out of the hole on the room side by about ¾ in. It will be such a tight fit that no child can dislodge it, and even an adult will probably have to use a pair of pliers to do so. Renew the length of dowel when it starts to become a loose fit.

Cleaning soot from house walls: There is no easy way of getting rid of years of accumulation of soot on house walls in industrial areas. First try hosing down, since this is a quick way of getting rid of any loose soot. Then, tackling a small area at a time, patiently scrub down the wall with a hard brush and a solution of household soda and bleach in hot water. Change the water regularly, otherwise you will merely be rubbing soot back into the building. Rinse off by hosing down.

Cleaning parquet floors: First get rid of old polish and the build-up of dirt by rubbing the floor thoroughly with pads of steel wool, dipped in turps. Have a supply of coarse rags ready to get rid of the excess spirit and dirt as you go. Finish the cleaning operation by scrubbing with hot detergent suds, then rinse with clear water, and allow it to dry, speeding up the process if you wish with dry rags. A medium and then a fine grade of sandpaper can be used to take any stains out of the wood. Finally, apply a polyurethane sealer, such as Ronseal hardglaze, in accordance with the makers' instructions.

Cleaning marble: Dissolve as many soda crystals as you can in an old cup filled with hot water, and then mix this solution with equal quantities of powdered whiting and pumice. Spread the paste thickly, and brush it well into the marble with a soft brush, then leave it overnight. Rinse away the compound and wash down the marble thoroughly in the morning. Repeat the whole process if it is still necessary. Removing any scratches in the marble is a job for a stonemason.

Painting over old tiles: When old wall tiles start to look faded and really down at heel, it is possible to paint over them. Wash them thoroughly, paying special attention to the grouting between the tiles. When they are dry, rub them with a medium grade emery cloth to dull the glaze. Dust them off and wipe them with a rag soaked in methylated spirits. As soon as this evaporates apply a coat of a good quality lacquer, such as Valspar, or Carson's lacquer. Further coats can be applied as needed to get a good gloss.

Scale in a kettle: It has been calculated that a deposit of $\frac{1}{16}$ in. on the bottom of a kettle can add as much as one minute to the time it takes to boil. This, in addition to the unpleasantness of having scale floating about in the teapot, shows that it is a problem worth trying to solve. The only way to stop scale forming in a kettle is, of course, to use nothing but soft water in it. That is a counsel of perfection that can be followed in a hard water area only by using a water softener, and this is an item of equipment that is not always found in British homes. Nevertheless, you can alleviate the nuisance.

Clean the inside of the kettle out once a day while you are doing the washing-up. Do not allow hot water to stand in it any longer than necessary – empty it completely the minute you have finished with it, taking care not to set it down on any hot cooker or cooking ring. Avoid keeping it simmering for long periods. Use the water in it immediately it starts to boil. Where the water is really hard and deposits form quickly, the old-fashioned remedies of placing sea shells, marbles, or pieces of canvas, stitched together in the water, are as good as any.

If deposits get really bad, they can be chipped away with a blunt knife or old screwdriver, providing you take care not to damage the metal casing of the kettle. As for chemical de-scaling, there are various formulas for mixing up a solvent, but the proprietary de-scalers are quite cheap, and they are safe as well as being effective. With these, the normal method is to pour warm water into the kettle, add de-scaler according to the makers' instructions, which will then start up a chemical action causing fizzing and bubbling. Remember to swish the liquid around so that it reaches the spout. When the action stops, you will know that de-scaling is complete. Follow very closely the makers' instructions about neutralizing afterwards.

Stains: In dealing with stains the first rule is to act quickly. Clean the affected spot immediately. Absorbent paper will soak up a lot of the liquid. If it does not get rid of it all, then use a solvent. The list below gives the best one to use for different types of stain. Always use a clean rag to apply the solvent – any old duster will not do – and, if possible, put a piece of absorbent paper behind the fabric.

There is always a danger that the fabric will not be sufficiently colour-fast and, as well as getting rid of the stain, the solvent will also remove some colour. So play safe, and test it first on a piece of spare fabric, or on a place where it will not show. Always use the solvents in a well ventilated room.

Alcoholic drinks, fruit juices and tea: Two teaspoonfuls of borax in half a pint of warm water. Swab the stain well, leave it for a few minutes, then rinse thoroughly.

Blood: Big S or Biotex. Make solution according to the makers' instructions. Dab it well and leave it to soak overnight. Next day rinse out.

Ball-point, indelible pencil, carbon paper: Dab with methylated spirits.

Car grease, face cream, hair oil, lipstick: K2R or Goddard's Dry Clean, according to the makers' recommendations.

Hair lacquer: Methylated spirit will remove this on fabric or mirrors, but it is not recommended for polished wood.

Grease on wallpaper: Try rubbing it with lumps of bread. Otherwise use Goddard's Dry Clean as directed.

Egg: Scrape off as much as possible, then dab on Beaucaire, Dabitoff, Thawpit or carbon tetrachloride.

Milk: Use the same solvents as for egg.

Nail varnish: Scrape off as much as you can, then dab on varnish remover. This will, however, damage acetates.

Bath stains: Rub them with vinegar, then rinse or try Venolite bath-stain remover.

Scorch marks: Sponge with two teaspoonfuls of borax in half a pint of warm water, then rinse.

Shoe polish: Dab with turpentine or methylated spirit.

Cleaning carpets: First give the carpet a thorough going-over with a vacuum cleaner, and, if the carpet is one that can be taken up, use the cleaner on both sides. Even after this, it is advisable, if possible, to take the carpet outside and beat it. When the carpet has been re-laid, it should be shampooed – Bex-Bissell make a Shampoo-Master that allows a person to do this without kneeling.

Otherwise, make a solution of a tablespoonful of 1001 to a pint of luke-warm water, and apply it with a soft brush or sponge. Wipe off excess foam and dirt with an old clean towel. Best results will be obtained by tackling small areas at a time. It is important to apply the cleaner evenly. Then use the vacuum cleaner once again when the carpet has dried properly.

Cleaning upholstery: So many materials are used for upholstery nowadays that it is difficult to be precise about cleaning instructions. Many plastics, which can be cleaned with a detergent, are used: some need a specific leather or upholstery cleaner. Of the fabrics, many are tough enough to be wet-cleaned like carpets, but some are not. It is best to seek the makers' advice, or experiment on a spot that will not be seen.

Cleaning metals: *Table Silver:* Wash it in liquid detergent, and then polish it with Duraglit Silver Polish. For badly tarnished items, pour a quart of water into an old saucepan, add half an ounce of borax, and bring the solution to the boil. Immerse the items in the solution but not, of course, anything such as knife handles – and keep it simmering for a few minutes. Then wash the silver in soapy water, and rinse, dry and polish it.

Pewter: Rub it with a chamois leather or any soft cloth after washing it in a solution of a liquid, rather than a powder, detergent.

Stainless steel: Use Goddard's Stainless Steel Care as directed.

Brass and copper: Long-neglected items can be given a new lease of life if they are rubbed with a mixture of salt and lemon juice. Wash them in soapy water, rinse and dry them, then clean them with Duraglit Metal Polish.

How to make loose covers: Even women who are first-rate dressmakers are put off by the thought of making loose covers. But really there is no need why this should be so, for loose cover making is not all that difficult. Remember

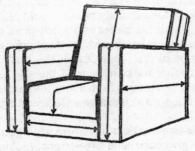

The component parts of a loose cover illustrated on an easy chair

you do not have to get the close fit of proper re-upholstery – even professional loose covers do not achieve that standard. The important point is to break the loose cover down into its component parts, and the sketch (page 39) shows these, with arrows indicating direction of the grain. Not all chairs are shaped exactly like this, but you should be able to grasp the principle from the sketch and adapt it to your own chairs.

Measure the component parts of the loose cover, making sure to check every measurement, since even mass-produced chairs are never as symmetrical as they seem. To these measurements, add a 1-in. seam allowance, except in the case of those edges (shown with a thick line in the sketch) that have to tuck into crevices, where the allowance should be 8 in. Now make life-size paper patterns from these measurements.

You need about five yards of 48-in. wide material for the average chair, but if there is a large-size pattern to match up, and especially if there is a large motif that has to be placed in the middle of the seat and back, you will need more. The paper pattern you have cut should help you to calculate just how much you need.

Cut the pieces out, and use a chalk line to mark the exact centre of the chair – on the outside back, top, inside back, seat and front border. Mark with tacking stitches the centre of the pieces, and pin these in position with the material inside out on the chair, matching centre to centre. Now you can mark with basting stitches exactly where the matching pieces should fit.

Unpin the pieces and stitch them together, piping the main seams with medium-thick piping cord, covered with strips of the fabric cut on the bias. For fitting and removal of the cover, one of the side seams on the outside back is left open from about four inches from the top, and is fitted with either press studs or a zip.

Making curtains: It is worth while going to a lot of trouble to give curtains a professional-looking finish. Curtains, especially when they are drawn and in a home with large windows, dominate a room, and good-looking curtains will make all the difference to the beauty and comfort of a home. Here are one or two general hints.

(1) There are two correct lengths – just above the sill, or 1 in. from the floor.

(2) Never economize on the width of your curtains. It is better to choose a cheaper fabric and give your curtains deep folds, than have an expensive fabric with hardly any folds at all.

(3) It is worth while lining curtains. They will then hang better in deeper, more luxurious folds, will wear longer, and make your home warmer.

(4) Always allow 1 in. on the length in case the curtains shrink later on, and include this allowance in the hem. This should be slip-stitched by hand rather than machined so that the length can be altered easily and quickly when necessary.

(5) Order more of a fabric that has a bold design, to give an allowance for matching the patterns on the different lengths.

(6) Finally, have the curtains cleaned frequently. They will then last a lot longer.

For the simplest curtain of all use Rufflette standard 1-in. tape and hooks, allowing 12 of these for each width of 48 in. used. Having decided the length, measure from

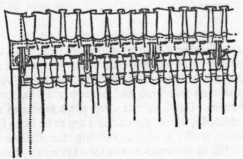

Allow 12 hooks to each width of 48 in.

the track, adding 5 to 8 in. for the hem and heading. For width allow at least $1\frac{1}{2}$ times the width of the curtain track. Add on $1\frac{1}{2}$ in. for any joins necessary and $1\frac{1}{2}$ in. for the side hems.

Machine the joins and slip-stitch the side hems. Turn over the top edge of the curtain $1\frac{1}{2}$ in., pin on the tape 1 in. from the top so that the raw edge is covered and knot the cord at one end. Machine all round the tape leaving the cords free. Pull up the cord to the required width and knot it. Do not cut the surplus cord, as this allows the curtains to be pulled flat for washing and ironing. Insert the hooks into the pockets, turn up the hem and slip-stitch it by hand.

Pencil Pleats: Use any weight of fabric, allowing twice the width of the curtain track, plus $1\frac{1}{2}$ in. for each side hem and $1\frac{1}{2}$ in. for joining seams where necessary. For the correct length, measure from the track adding 4 in. for the heading and 4 in. for the hem. Rufflette Regis tape is used – the same length as you have width of fabric – and standard hooks.

Machine the seams and hem the sides, then turn down the top edge $\frac{5}{8}$ in. and tack it. Take the tape (making sure that the pockets are at the bottom) and pin it flush to the top edge of the curtain. Machine it in place. Knot the cords at one end, and from the other pull the two cords evenly to the required width. Insert the hooks into the pockets every 3 to 4 in. Turn up the hem and slip-stitch it.

Pinch Pleats: Decide on the length and measure from the track, allowing 4 in. for the bottom hem and 4 in. for the heading. Choose a plain, heavy-woven fabric or velvet and allow $2\frac{1}{2}$ times the width of the track. Add on $1\frac{1}{2}$ in. for each side hem and a further $1\frac{1}{2}$ in. for each joining seam. Use Rufflette deep pleat tape and short-stemmed hooks, unless the curtains are to be hung from a ceiling-fixed track, in which case long-stemmed hooks are needed. The same hooks can be used for single, double or triple pleats by inserting the prongs correctly into the pockets of the tape. For single pleats insert only the two inner prongs, for double, use three prongs and for triple pleats use all four prongs.

Hem the sides and machine the joins where necessary. Turn over the top edge of the curtain $\frac{5}{8}$ in. and tack it. Pin on the tape so that it is flush with the top edge of the curtain. Machine all round the outer edge of the tape, avoiding the pockets. Insert the hooks, turn up the hem and slip-stitch it.

Ruched heading: Allow at least $1\frac{1}{2}$ times the width of the track if a heavy fabric is being used; twice the width for a light one. Add $1\frac{1}{2}$ in. for each side hem and $1\frac{1}{2}$ in. for any necessary seams. Decide on the length, and measure from the track, adding 6 to 8 in. for heading and hem. You will also need Rufflette standard curtain tape –

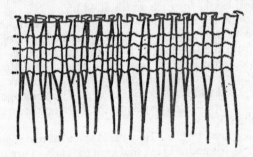

Pleats and ruched headings using Rufflette tape

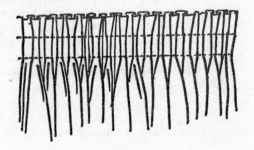

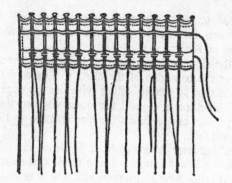

Pull the ends of the cords free when lining curtains

the length will be three times the curtain width – and 12 standard hooks for each width of 48 in.

Machine the seams, and hem the side seams by hand. Turn over the top edge 1½ in. and pin one length of tape 1 in. from the top so that it covers the raw edge. Now pin two more lengths, one below the other. Machine knot the cords at one end, pull up the other end evenly to the required width and knot this end. The hooks go into the upper tape – one every 3 to 4 in. Turn up the hem and slip-stitch it.

Lining your curtains: Take the tape and at one edge pull free the cords about 1½ in., and knot the ends. Turn under the end of the tape, including the knot, to neaten the edge and stitch. With the right side of the lining, and the tape uppermost, insert the raw edge of the lining between the tape, pin it in position and machine-stitch it. Pull up the cords so that the lining is the same width as the curtain. Remove one by one the hooks on the curtain and insert them first into a pocket on the lining tape and then back into the curtain.

Home Decorating

Order of Work: First must come the preparation – which is the word the professional uses to describe the washing down, paint stripping, sanding, removal of wallpaper and the general getting ready of a surface for the decorative finish. The order for this is to start with the ceilings, followed by the walls, the doors, and finally any other woodwork such as window-frames, skirting boards and door-frames. There is one important difference between washing down walls and woodwork prior to redecorating, and washing surfaces that are in good order, and merely need cleaning. In the former instance, it is better to start at the top of the wall and work downwards, although no great harm would be done if you worked the other way about. But when walls are to be washed merely to clean them it is vital that you start at the bottom and work upwards. If a start is made at the top, dribbles of water will run over the dirt on the lower parts of the wall that have still to be cleaned, and no amount of subsequent washing and rubbing will obliterate completely the marks that these make.

If the ceilings and walls are to have a paint finish, then as a general rule this should be applied next, followed by the paint on the door, and lastly the rest of the woodwork. There is, however, one exception to this rule, and that is

45

when very dark and very light paints are to be used in the same room. Where the two colours meet, the joining line should, to give a good appearance, be straight and neat. The technical term for creating this line is "cutting-in". There is no need to do the job of cutting-in twice – i.e. once for each colour. The light paint should be applied first, even if this means painting the walls before the ceiling, and the doors and skirting board before the walls. The light colour can be allowed to stray on to the area that will later receive the darker paint. The cutting-in should be attempted only when the darker paint is being applied, because this will easily obliterate the light paint. Do not, of course, attempt to apply the darker paint until the light paint is completely dry.

If a ceiling is to be painted and the walls papered, the ceiling and the woodwork should be painted before the paper is applied. There are two reasons for this. First, it minimizes the chances of paint being splashed on to the paper; and second, there is no need to do any cutting-in when paint on the ceiling, door-frames, window-frames and skirting board is being applied. This can be allowed to stray on to the plaster, because when the paper is trimmed to a good fit later on it will disguise any inaccuracies in the painting. There is one word of warning necessary. In sizing the walls, prior to papering, it is important to avoid splashing the painted areas with size. Any splashes that do occur should be wiped off immediately with a damp rag.

It cannot be stressed too strongly that preparation is the most important part of the whole decorating process. Preparation is also the least interesting aspect of the job: it is tiring, time-consuming and boring. Yet the finished result will be no better than the amount of work that is put into the preparation. Modern decorating materials are superb, but they cannot work miracles. They must be given a chance, and this means applying them to a surface that is fit to receive them. Even if they look good at first, they will not last long on a badly prepared surface. The aim of preparation is to make a surface flat, smooth, dry, clean, firm and, perhaps most important of all, free from flaking material.

Non-washable distemper: This is now rarely used, but it is still possible to come across it in old property. Unfortunately, it has to be removed completely, and doing this can be a tiresome job. The best tool to use is an old distemper brush, but a constant supply of rags will do in its place. Thoroughly wet the distemper, working on about a yard at a time, and work it up into a sludge, when it can be removed. If several coats of the distemper have been applied one on top of the other, a broad, flat scraper can be used to get rid of the slime. Finally, give the surface a good sanding to get rid of any distemper that remains after this treatment.

Emulsion paints and washable distempers: Any loose or flaking material should be removed with a broad flat scraper. Then the wall should be washed with a solution of detergent or cleansing agent, and given a thorough rinsing, if the makers' instructions call for this. When washing down, work on about a square yard at a time, and begin with a series of whirling, circular movements, the point of which is to loosen the dirt. Remove the dirt with a final series of straight strokes, wringing out the rag into the bucket of water constantly, and changing the water as soon as it gets very dirty. The process of washing down may have to be repeated a few times in rooms that have not been touched for some time. Finally, give the surface a light sanding down with a fine glasspaper.

Oil paints on walls: Under this heading is meant gloss paints, enamels, flat and eggshell paints. The treatment is similar to that for emulsion paints, with the proviso that the final sanding down is more vital, especially with a high gloss. This sheen prevents later decorative surfaces – whether they be paint or paper – from adhering properly.

Oil paints on woodwork: A lot depends on the condition of this. If it is in good shape and redecoration is to be carried out merely for the sake of a colour change, or to freshen-up a surface that has lost its first pristine newness, then a washing down, followed by a sanding with first a medium then a fine glasspaper, should be sufficient. If there are a few odd bits of flaking paint, then these should be removed with a scraper. Areas of paint adjacent to bare wood should be sanded and "feathered" down so that the change from paint to bare timber is more gradual. If there are extensive defects, such as large areas of bare timber, lots of flaking material, or areas of crazed, mosaic-like paint, then it is better to strip the whole area bare.

Paint stripping: The cheapest way is to use a blowlamp – although this should never be applied to metal. The hot flame of the blowlamp is allowed to play on the timber, and it soon causes the paint, no matter how many layers there are, to bubble up. It is then a simple matter to remove the paint with a scraper. The flame should never be allowed to stay too long in one particular spot, or it will char the wood. If the charring is not too bad, however, it can easily be removed with glasspaper. Special care has to be taken on window-frames, because if the hot flame touches the glass it will crack it. Because of this, it may well be that it is inadvisable for the amateur to use this method of stripping on window-frames, although he can use a sheet of metal as a shield, and it will usually give sufficient protection. Beware, however, that the metal does not get so hot that it burns the hand. Another danger is that lumps of hot burning paint will fall on to the floor causing damage, so a protective sheet should be laid down near the work.

Those people, however, who are afraid to use a blowlamp – and it can seem quite a terrifying instrument at first, although the modern types are safe enough, especially the new gas-type blowlamps which require, literally, only a match to light them – should use a paint-stripping fluid. This is applied to the work by brush, and it has the same bubbling effect as the blowlamp. The paint is then removed with a scraper. The process may have to be repeated several times, if there are many coats of paint on the work, as there undoubtedly will be for the surface to be in bad condition. Many proprietary paint strippers are on the market. Always follow the makers' instructions closely, especially about neutralizing the surface afterwards, otherwise you may find the stripper affecting the new paint when you apply it.

The scrapers to use are a broad flat one for the large areas, and a triangular one, known as a shave hook, for getting into awkward corners. In addition, there are several types shaped for dealing with different kinds of moulding.

After the paint has been removed, the surface should be given a thorough sanding with first a medium then a fine glasspaper.

Paint stripping on metal: As already stated, a blowlamp should never be used on metal, because the heat will cause it to twist and distort, and might even pierce a hole in it, if it is delicate enough. On tough metals, such as the iron found on exterior drain-pipes and guttering, a wire brush – especially one used in an electric drill – will get rid of paintwork that is adhering badly. Otherwise, a paint stripper is the safest method.

Handles and catches: Sometimes these are to be painted along with the door or window-frame, sometimes they are in decorative metal, and are meant to be left in their natural state. In the latter case, it can be a great nuisance having to get round them during both the preparation and the final painting. There is no doubt at all that it is quicker in the long run to take them off, even if you have to replace them each night on a window or outside door, for the sake of security. Most of them can, with a little care, be replaced even while the paint is still wet.

Wallpaper: On balance it is probably best to strip off any existing wallpaper on the walls. If the paper is in bad condition it is essential to do so. If it is in good condition it is not, strictly speaking, vital. New wallpaper and emulsion paint (but not an oil paint) can be applied on top of existing paper. You do run several risks, however, by not stripping it first. Any imperfections in the paper will show through the new paper – unevenness, bad joins, etc. As for emulsion paint, this is less tricky. In fact, on walls where the plaster is not in too good a condition, the professional decorator often puts up a lining paper, (i.e. a plain white paper, with no pattern on it whatsoever) before he uses the paint. On wallpaper that has been up for some time, there is just the risk, however, that the paint will break down the glue, and cause the paper to come away from the walls. A strong, boldly coloured pattern might also show through a pale emulsion paint. Carry out a test in an unobtrusive corner, or on a piece of spare paper. And the paint might also cause the colouring in the paper to run.

Stripping off wallpaper is not a difficult task. The first step is to give the paper a thorough soaking, with either plain water or a proprietary wallpaper stripper, such as Polystrippa. After about fifteen minutes, give it another liberal dousing. In about twenty minutes the wallpaper glue should have softened, and removal of the paper can begin.

Take a broad flat scraper, start at the bottom, and try to pull the paper off the wall in long strips. Take care, however, that the scraper does not damage the underlying plaster, for any scratches or holes will have to be made good later. There will be less likelihood of damage if the scraper is held at an acute angle to the wall. When all the paper has been removed, there may still be bits of old size or glue clinging to the wall, and ready to show up through the final finish. These can be got rid of if the surface is given a final wash down with a scrubbing brush and luke-warm water. A final light sanding with fine glasspaper will mean that the wall is ready for the final finish.

Stripping wallpaper in very old houses: The foregoing remarks are all very well for houses with a sound plaster surface under the paper. In very old homes, however, the plaster may be old, crumbly, and ready to disintegrate. In fact, the paper will be the only thing that is preventing the plaster from sagging and falling to the floor. Tap the surface of the wall in a few places, and listen for the sound. You will be able to tell from this whether it seems sound and hard, or weak and crumbly. If you fear the worst, there are two alternatives. A decision can be reached to apply the new decorative surface on top of the existing paper, bearing in mind all the cautions given in the previous section. On the other hand, plaster that is in such bad condition is going to have to be renewed, and probably sooner than later, and since the room needs completely redecorating anyway it is as good a time as any to do it. Replastering is not, however, a job that the unskilled amateur can tackle properly.

Filling cracks and holes: When all other preparation is complete, the surface should be examined for cracks and holes. These need to be filled for a perfect finish. The best material for doing so is a cellulose filler, such as Polyfilla; the technique is to rake out loose material, then push the filler in with a putty knife, leaving the surface slightly proud. It can then be sanded down flat with fine glasspaper. Deep and large holes should be filled in two stages, a half at a time. Hair-line cracks are the big problem when it comes to filling, for, no matter how many you deal with, there always seems to be another and yet another waiting to be done. The fact is, however, that the more you fill, the better will be the finished result. Even if the paint or paper covers them up when newly applied, they will eventually start to show through.

Types of paint: Knotting is the first material you apply to bare woodwork. You cover with it any knots that are showing, and it prevents the resinous substance from "weeping" out and spoiling the finished result. You should apply knotting especially on outdoor woodwork, for the heat of the sun may cause the resin to swell up and seep through the paintwork. Indoors, particularly if the knots look dry, it is not strictly essential to use knotting.

Primers: A primer is, as its name implies, the paint that you apply first (apart from knotting on woodwork) to give a base for subsequent coats to grip on. There are different primers for different substances – wood, metal, even bare plaster in new houses – and these are not interchangeable. Again, it is more important to apply primer out of doors than inside, and an exterior rust-inhibiting primer for metal is of special importance.

Gloss paint: A very tough, durable paint that is used for interior and exterior woodwork, and was for many years the first paint choice for use in heavy-duty areas such as kitchens and bathrooms. It has, however, a hard shiny surface and if there are large areas of it, it tends to encourage condensation. It is also not so easy to apply in large areas as other paints that have been introduced on the market since then. For these two reasons it is not now so popular for wall use as it was.

Undercoats: These are preparatory coats for gloss paints. You apply them before the gloss on top of a primer and knotting, on surfaces which, although not so bad as to need a primer, are still in a poor condition, and even on top of surfaces that are in pretty good shape if you want to make a colour change from dark to light. If, however, you are painting merely to freshen up a surface that is otherwise in good condition, or to change from a very light to a much darker colour, you can dispense with the undercoat stage.

Polyurethane paints: These are a new introduction on the market, and they have a much more brilliant surface than gloss paints, and they are tougher. They are, however, much more expensive. You might, though, think the expense justified to get their clear, shining brilliance on, for instance, a piece of living-room furniture you had made or were renovating; and you might be happy to pay the extra to get their toughness on kitchen cabinets or their scuff-resistance on skirting boards. They do not need undercoats.

Flat paints: Another name for these is eggshell paints, because it is exactly that which their soft, flat surface brings to mind. Like gloss paints, they are oil-based, but they are not so tough as a gloss, and are not suited to outdoor use. Many people, however, prefer their soft texture for interior woodwork and walls, and they are not so likely to cause condensation in kitchens and bathrooms. Flat paints do not have an undercoat; you merely use as many finishing coats as are needed.

Thixotropic paints: Many gloss and flat paints are also thixotropic – i.e. instead of being a liquid they are a solid, jelly-like substance. When you press a brush on it, the paint temporarily becomes liquid, and the bristles can be loaded with paint, then it solidifies again until you start to spread it on the surface. There is only one point to all this – the paint will not drip like a liquid does and splash about as you paint.

Emulsions: These were one of the great innovations of the early post-war years, right at the spearhead of the great do-it-yourself home decorating movement that grew up at that time. They have come a long way since then. At one time they were thought of as being suitable only for living-rooms where they would not have to withstand much wear and tear. Now you can get emulsion paints to be used anywhere – kitchen, bathroom, even out of doors

53

– and they are highly washable. They are, though, essentially wall paints, and unsuitable for woodwork.

Cement paints: These usually come in powder form ready to be mixed in water. They are the cheapest way of treating large areas of external wall, such as rendering, and for many years were the only really practical way of doing so. They still have their uses provided you do not ask the impossible of them and put them in situations for which they are clearly unsuitable. Always follow the manufacturers' specifications in this.

Stone paints: Although more expensive than cement paints, they give really strong protection to external walls. They can be used on stucco, cement rendering, pebble dash, Tyrolean finish, brick and stone. Always, however, follow the makers' ruling about this, and never use one of these paints in a situation where he advises you not to.

Specialist paints: In addition to the more common paints there is a whole range of specialized paints for specific jobs, including step and tile paints, lino paints, bath enamels, celluloses, and heat-resistant paints.

How to paint: Oil paints are the most difficult to apply. You cannot just "slosh" them on and hope for the best, or you will get unsightly runs. There is a simple technique of applying them to large vertical areas, however, and these sketches show it. You charge the brush and make a series of vertical stripes spaced about a brush width apart. With an empty brush, make a series of strokes at right angles to these, spreading the paint fully across the area. Finally with a dry brush make a series of very light strokes vertically in the original direction with your brush only just kissing the paint – a process known as laying off. Tackle adjacent areas in the same way, taking your strokes well into patches you have already painted so that there is not a clearly visible line between them. Continue

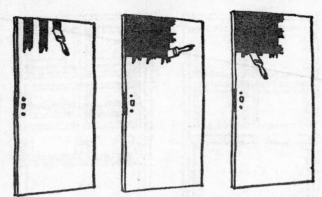

There is a simple technique for applying paint to large vertical areas

in this way until you have covered the whole area you wish to paint.

This technique does not, naturally, apply to long thin areas, such as skirting boards, door- or window-frames and glazing bars. Here you must resist the temptation to use too much paint, and always be certain to brush it out fully, so that there is no chance it will run. On glazing bars, the point that worries the amateur is getting a lot of paint on the glass, which can be difficult to remove afterwards. If you cannot trust the steadiness of your hands, then use a masking tape. Sellotape do one, which consists of Kraft paper with a non-aggressive adhesive backing, that allows it to be easily stripped off the glass when the job is done, leaving a nice clean break between glazing bar and timber.

There is also another Sellotape that is very useful to the amateur decorator at this juncture, and that is Sellotape-X, a plasticised cloth tape with a very powerful adhesive. Use it to cover up the gap that occurs between skirting board and floor as the timber shrinks, for not only does this look ugly, but it also lets through droughts as well.

Emulsion paints do not require the same care in

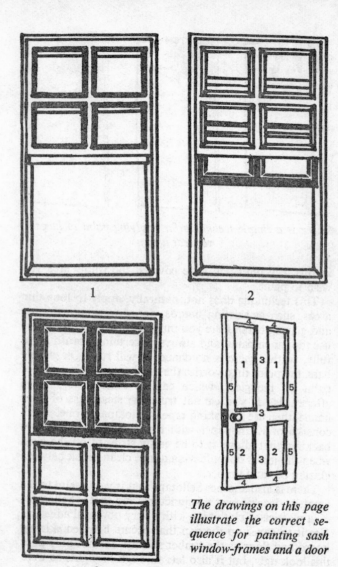

The drawings on this page illustrate the correct sequence for painting sash window-frames and a door

application as the oil-bound paints, since they do not run in the same way. All you need to do is make sure you spread them evenly over the surface, and that you do not leave any spots uncovered.

With polyurethane paints, too, the technique is slightly different, because this also does not need brushing out to the same extent. You should apply the paint to the surface with minimum brushwork, and re-charge the brush as soon as you feel it start to drag.

Painting sash window-frames: Push the inner sash, which should normally be at the bottom, to the top, and pull down the outer sash so that half of it is showing. Paint all the woodwork you can now see. When this is finished pull the inner sash down to the bottom, push the outer one up, and finish painting it. The inner one can then be tackled in the normal way.

How to hang wallpaper: If you do not like the large areas of one unbroken colour that painted walls give you, then wallpaper, with its wide choice of patterns and styles, is for you. There are the ordinary grades of wallpaper, washable papers, and the more expensive vinyl coated papers that are so tough you can even scrub them. Here are the basic steps in simple wallpaper hanging:

You will need these tools: a pair of steps; buckets; 3-ft. rule; pencil; 6-in. pasting brush; paper-hanging brush for smoothing out paper; 1-in. roller for smoothing out seams; long-bladed scissors; a piece of string weighted to act as a plumb-line and bob; and a pasting board – if you do not have a table big enough, get a piece of hardboard 6 × 2 ft., strengthen it by nailing it to a framework of 2 × 1-in. battens on the back, and rest it on any convenient objects.

Measure the height of the wall, and cut a piece of paper to length, allowing 6 in. for trimming on a small pattern, as much as 1 ft. on a large one. Put the piece face upwards on the pasting table, and use it as a guide for cutting the

It is best to paste wallpaper on a table 6 x 2 ft.

*Paste from the centre and work outwards,
making sure the edges are well covered*

*Make a support across
the bucket for the brush*

*Carry the folded paper
carefully to the wall*

remaining pieces to length. Now mix the size in the bucket and apply it to the walls with the pasting brush. Then mix the paste in the same bucket. If you use a cellulose paste such as Polycell, it can also be used for sizing in a weaker mixture. Turn the paper upside down on the pasting board, and paste one end of it, allowing as much as necessary of the other end to overhang. Paste from the centre and work outwards, making sure the edges are well covered. Fold the half you have just pasted in towards the centre, move the paper along the table, and paste the other half, folding this too when you have finished.

When you are hanging paper, you should always work away from the main source of light – let us assume that in this case it will be from right to left.

Measure the width of the paper from the top right-hand corner of the wall, and drop the plumb-line from this point, marking its position on the wall with a pencil.

Carry the folded paper to the wall, mount the steps, take hold of the top edge of the paper and it will just fall out of its folds. Bring the left edge up against the plumb-line, allow the overlap at the top edge for trimming, and smooth the paper with the brush. With the back of the scissors score a line on the paper where it meets the top of the wall, draw the paper back, and cut it to size. Repeat this process at skirting-board level.

Carry on hanging lengths of paper, until you come to the end of a wall, where it will almost certainly be necessary to cut a piece to fit. Measure how wide a piece of paper is needed, and cut it from the standard roll, making it slightly oversize. Paste and fold it in the normal way, and hang it as you have done the other pieces. With the back of the scissors score where it meets the angle of the adjacent wall, draw it away and cut it with the scissors. In other words, you are using an adaptation of the method used for trimming the paper to the skirting board and ceiling.

When you come to a doorway, press the paper with the

scissors against the door-frame, draw the paper away and cut it to width as far as the height of the door. Now press the top portion of the paper to the wall, score where it meets the top of the frame, draw the paper away and cut it to size. Treat a fireplace in a similar way.

Flush plate electrical switches can be removed to allow you to paper the wall (don't forget to switch off at the mains first), but you cannot do this with old-fashioned surface-mounted switches. The technique is to pierce the paper with your scissors at the centre of the switch and cut back away from this in the fashion of a star. Press the paper gently round the switch to get a mark to which you can trim. Peel back the segments and cut them to size, finally smoothing the paper into place.

If, when you come to the top end of a wall, you intend to paper the return wall in the same material, cut a length $\frac{1}{2}$ in. oversize, and turn the surplus on to the return wall. Now take the spare length you have cut from the piece, and hang it on the return wall, allowing it to overlap where the corner is not true.

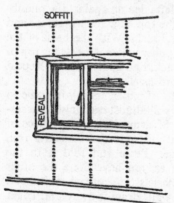
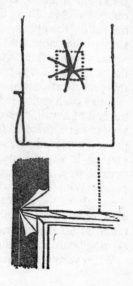

These sketches illustrate the methods for papering around a window, a door-frame, and an electric-light switch

60

As for a window, you find the centre point and drop a plumb-line from it. On either side of this you hang short lengths of paper and carry them underneath the soffit, trimming them up against the window-frame. If the wall is so out of true that the paper under the soffit looks crooked, you will have to accomplish this operation with two pieces of paper, that on the wall overlapping the soffit piece by $\frac{1}{2}$ in. Carry on in this way until you come to the full-length piece. Hang this to a plumb-line at its outside edge, and cut it at the top of the window opening so that it will turn into the reveal; at the bottom trim it to go round the window-sill. Turn the paper into the reveal, and trim it against the window-frame, if it is long enough. If not, you will have to hang a separate piece in the reveal, allowing the long piece to overlap it by $\frac{1}{2}$ in. Under the soffit, there will be one separate piece of paper still to hang, going under the edges of adjacent paper.

How much do you need? The covering capacity of paint varies enormously according to how porous the surface is, but the following is a rough guide:

Primers: 1 quart will cover 130 sq. ft. of porous or 240 sq. ft. of non-porous surface.

Undercoats: 1 quart will cover 220 to 260 sq. ft.

Finishing coats: 1 quart will cover about 200 sq. ft.

In all the above cases, you can reckon you need $\frac{1}{4}$ pint to cover one side of a door and its frame.

Emulsions: 1 quart will cover about 200 sq. ft.

The following table shows how to estimate the amount of wallpaper you need:

Height of walls from skirting	Measurement in feet around walls, including normal doors and windows									
	28	32	36	40	44	48	52	56	60	64
7 ft. 6 in.–	Number of rolls									
8 ft.	4	4	5	5	6	6	7	8	8	9
8 ft.– 8 ft. 6 in.	4	5	5	6	6	7	7	8	8	9
8 ft. 6 in.– 9 ft.	4	5	5	6	6	7	8	8	9	9

Ceiling paper	Number of rolls
Up to 28 ft. measurement around four sides of room	1
Between 30 ft. to 40 ft. measurement around four sides of room	2
Between 42 ft. to 48 ft. measurement around four sides of room	3
Between 52 ft. to 58 ft. measurement around four sides of room	4
Between 60 ft. to 64 ft. measurement around four sides of room	5

Cleaning paint-brushes: First get rid of all the surplus paint on the brush. Work it off on an old piece of timber, otherwise, scrape the surplus paint off with the back of an old knife or a thin piece of wood. The brush should then be dipped in a jar of a liquid that is a solvent for the paint (see table below) and agitated briskly, to loosen the paint. Particular attention should be paid to the stock of the brush, where paint particles can gather. Then the brush should be washed in a solution of soap or mild detergent in water, until it is thoroughly clean. It should then be rinsed, and wrapped in a piece of old newspaper and squeezed, to dry it out thoroughly, then put away and stored. Thread a length of string through the hole in the brush handle (you will have to drill a hole if there is not one there already) and hang it from a hook. As an alternative, containers such as the Brush Bank which hold the brush in a tin of preserving fluid are now available.

The following are the solvents for various types of paint:

Gloss paints, enamels and flat paints: Paraffin, turpentine, white spirit (often referred to as turps substitute) or a proprietary cleaner such as Polyclens.

Cellulose paint: Amyl acetate, mixed with wood naptha

for economy, or thinners supplied by the maker of the paint.

Rubber paint: Petrol – but do not use it indoors.

Emulsion paint: Water – provided it is used before the paint has set really hard. When dry, try white spirit or a proprietary cleaner. If these fail alcohol or meths may be more successful.

Distemper: Water – once again provided it is used before the paint has dried. Some dry distempers can be removed with a solution of weak vinegar; others respond to treatment with petrol or paraffin.

Exterior painting: The basic principles of exterior painting are just the same as those already given for indoors. There is, however, one major difference. The man working out of doors has the weather to contend with. These points should, therefore, be noted.

The best time to paint out of doors is in early autumn. By then the sun's rays, which can be just as harmful to newly applied paint as can more inclement weather, are past their strongest; the heat of summer should have dried out any dampness present in the woodwork; and this is normally the driest time of the year in Great Britain.

It is not, however, always possible to tackle exterior painting at the ideal time. Many people use their spare week's summer holiday for this. Those doing the work in high summer should, wherever they can, always follow the sun, rather than precede it. They should work on areas on which the sun has finished shining, and are now in the shade.

Paint should never be applied to wet surfaces. In this context, it is, quite rightly, usual to think of dampness as coming from rain. There is, however, another important source, and that is dew. Work should, therefore, not be started too early in the morning before the dew has cleared, and it should not continue too long into the dusk of a summer night. The drying process can always be speeded up by wiping the surfaces with a piece of old towelling.

If the preparation leaves any surfaces bare, they should be covered with paint before work is finished for the day. Otherwise dampness may get into timber, and metal may be rusted, if there is a fall of rain or a heavy dew during the night.

It is possible to make some short cuts in interior painting, but it is inviting disaster to try to do so out of doors. All bare knots should be covered with knotting, bare surfaces should be primed, and an undercoat put on before the top coat.

The initial coats such as knotting, primers, and undercoats cannot withstand the ravages of the weather. Therefore, whilst it may be a good method of working indoors to do all the priming in a room, then all the undercoating at one go and all the top coat at the same time, this is not so out of doors. These weaker paints should be covered as soon as possible.

Working on ladders: The other big difference about outdoor work is that, except in the case of a bungalow, a lot of the work will have to be done high above ground level. Here are some tips to ensure safety.

When raising the ladder, get a helper to stand at one end with his foot firmly on the bottom rung, or jam this end up against a wall. Pick up the opposite end of the ladder, and face your helper. Raise the ladder above the head, with your arms outstretched, and walk towards your helper, raising the ladder all the time. For lowering the ladder the procedure is reversed.

When carrying the ladder it is best to keep it upright. The hand nearest the ladder should go outside it and hold a rung at waist level. The other hand should be on the opposite side, holding a rung at head level.

One danger is that the bottom of the ladder will slide away from the wall while you are still on it. If it is on soft ground drive a stake into the earth and tie the ladder to this.

On concrete or other hard surfaces, there may be a convenient point such as a drain-pipe to which the ladder can be tied. Perhaps it can be fixed to a window-frame. It may be possible to reach a staircase post by passing a rope through a letter-box opening. Another method on concrete is to place a piece of sacking under the feet of the ladder, so that the surface will be less slippery.

If you own the ladder yourself, as distinct from having hired it, use a clear wood preservative on it, rather than paint. Any defects will then be more readily visible. These should be repaired immediately.

Never attempt to stretch too far on the top of a ladder just to save yourself the trouble of getting down to move it.

If you stretch out to open or close a window and a lot of pressure seems to be called for, beware. You might find that the window will stay put, and the ladder will move, throwing you to the ground. Better to get down, move the ladder nearer, and close or open the window in safety.

Ceramic tiles: Fixing ceramic wall tiles in place used to be thought of as a highly skilled job, beyond the capabilities of the home handyman. Two developments have changed this. In the first place, manufacturers started to produce a whole range of thinner tiles – $\frac{1}{4}$ in. thick or less, as compared with the $\frac{1}{2}$ in., or even more, of the old tiles. These tiles were not, originally, produced with the do-it-yourself man in mind, but it was soon seen that they would be a terrific boon to him, because they would make it so much easier for him to cut the tiles.

The second development was a new range of first-class, easy-to-use and long-lasting ceramic tile adhesives, which has made the old sand-and-cement method right out of date. With these two factors, wall tiling becomes a job that anyone can tackle with confidence.

There are one or two subsidiary aids in the range of do-it-yourself tiles. For instance, it is important that the tiles should be neatly and equally spaced on the wall. One manufacturer makes this simple by fixing spacer lugs to the sides of his tile. They are not visible in the finished result, but they ensure even spacing. When using tiles without spacer lugs, tear up into small pieces the cartons in which the tiles have been delivered, and insert the pieces between the tiles, leaving them in place until the adhesive has set. Alternately, a series of matchsticks could be used – preferably after they have been struck. Another manufacturer – Polycell – makes very thin tiles that have a slight bevel on all edges. This obviates the need for ordering specially shaped tiles with a so-called "bull-nosed" edge, to be used on the top row of the tiling, or even a tile with a bevel on two sides for the top and outer edges.

Preparation: As with all aspects of home decorating, the preparation is very important. It is no use fixing good-quality tiles with a first-class adhesive to a loose and flaking surface, because the tiles will merely come away with the bits of flaking material. All loose stuff should, therefore, be removed with a broad, flat paint scraper, or even a stiff brush in very bad cases.

The tiles will cover any minor holes and cracks, but if there are any defects in the wall that would stop the ultimate result from being flat and level, they should be filled in. A mixture of one part of sand to three parts of cement can be used for this. Or, if there is not a lot of making good necessary, a filler such as Polyfilla can be used. Where a wall is in really bad condition hardboard can first of all be fixed in place, and the tiles stuck to this. Never, however, fix tiles to an unstable material – such as timber – that will expand and contract as it absorbs and sheds moisture, for the movement will crack the tiles. Finally, the surface should be clean and dry before operations begin.

Simple tiling: A wash-basin splashback is a good example of how to carry out simple wall tiling. This is, in fact, one of the simplest and easiest of tiling jobs, but the principles will be the same for a whole variety of similar tasks. First decide on the area you wish the splashback to occupy. Its width can be approximately the same as the basin, or it can be wider. Its height is a matter of preference. Go along to your supplier and tell him the area you wish to cover, and he will sell you the correct number of tiles, with perhaps one or two extras in case of breakages, for most makers warn you that tiles ordered at a subsequent date cannot be guaranteed an exact colour match of those you have bought earlier. Set the tiles out on the floor in the shape they will occupy, and at this stage be prepared to adjust slightly, if at all possible, the area you had in mind so that you will not have to cut any tiles.

The adhesive will stop the tiles from falling away from the walls even before it has set. It will not, however, prevent them from sliding down the wall to finish up on the floor. Therefore, something has to be placed on the wall to stop this. The back ledge of the wash-basin will serve this purpose, but, if the splashback is to extend beyond this, then timber battens (2 × 1 in. is a suitable size) must be fixed to the wall on each side of the basin, and level with the top. Since these battens are merely temporary, there is no need to make a very good fixing to the wall. On good, sound plaster they can be merely tacked in place.

Now read the manufacturers' instructions on the tin of adhesive. Some makers recommend that the adhesive be applied to the wall, and the tiles merely placed in position. If this is the case, draw the area of the splashback on the wall lightly with a pencil and apply the adhesive. The maker will probably suggest that you "comb" the adhesive with a special tool that has a serrated edge, and is supplied with the tiles. This allows the adhesive to get a better grip on the tiles. Other makers suggest that the adhesive be "buttered" on to the back of the tiles, and others specify merely five spots of adhesive placed on the back at strategic positions.

Now begin to place the tiles on to the wall, adopting whichever method of using the adhesive and spacing the tiles that is recommended. When you have finished, allow the adhesive to set properly, and you can begin the operation known as "grouting". If you look at tiling carried out by a professional, you will see that the tiles are not jammed up together, but are spaced slightly apart. There is a reason for this. Ceramics are a living material and they need room to expand and contract as they "breathe" – so never be tempted to think you can do without this spacing.

To neaten the joins – and also to stop dirt from gathering there, which would be unhygienic as well as unsightly – the gap is filled with a white compound. This is known as grouting – both the material and the operation of fixing it in place – and it is probably the most difficult operation for the amateur in tiling. Mix the grouting compound, and start to insert it. If the maker does not supply a special tool for this, then improvise one from a thin sheet of card, or use a paint scraper or putty knife. Try to work as neatly as you can while doing this, but have a wet rag handy to wipe up the considerable amounts of compound that will undoubtedly get on to the face of the tiles. When the compound has set, the splashback is ready for use.

Whole-wall tiling: The beginner who has successfully tackled a simple piece of tiling, such as the splashback described above, will undoubtedly want to go on to more ambitious projects, like tiling the whole of a wall, or even a room. In truth, there is really only one extra skill involved, and that is cutting a tile to size, for you will find it necessary to do this when tiling a whole wall.

Cutting a tile: Cutting a tile is not really a difficult process, but it is a knack that has to be mastered. The beginner who is trying to acquire the skill for the first time should be prepared to break quite a few tiles to start with – it might be even as many as one or two dozen – but just when he is starting to lose heart, and think he will have to call in a tradesman to do the tiling for him, he will suddenly find that he has learned the trick.

There are only two pieces of equipment necessary for cutting a tile, and they are an instrument for scoring the surface, and a straightedge. For scoring, some people use a glass-cutter with a wheel, but a proper tiler's spike is to be preferred. The straightedge can be anything you like – a piece of hardwood of dimensions something like $1 \times \frac{1}{4}$ in. would do, and so would a metal 1-ft. ruler.

The important part of the operation is to carry out the scoring properly. First measure what size the cut tile has to be. Incidentally, it is worth while stressing here that you cannot rely on the walls of a room being square, and it is essential to measure the top and bottom of the tile. Mark the tile, on the side away from the glaze, with a sharp pencil, or the spike, where the cuts have to be made. Place the tile on a flat surface at a convenient height – a woodworking bench or kitchen table are ideal. Place the straightedge in position flat on the tile so that it coincides at each end with the marks you have made. Put the spike hard up against the straightedge and draw it firmly and surely across the tile's face, so that it cuts right through the glaze.

This operation should be performed with just one stroke – it is bad practice to keep drawing the spike across the face of the tile, for this will more than likely result in several smaller score marks, rather than one wide one. And it is essential that the glaze on the edge of the tile, where it is slightly bevelled, should be cut through just as surely and cleanly as the face.

If the waste portion of the tile is a fair size – say more than 1 in. – place the tile face upwards on the right-hand edge of the bench so that just the waste portion is overhanging. Hold the tile firmly in place with your left hand, place your right over the waste, and press down on it firmly and positively, but without using brute force. The tile should then snap cleanly along the score line. Even if it does not do so right away, it will after you have practised a few times. As an alternative to this method, some authorities suggest that the tile be placed on a matchstick or pencil that is right under the score mark, instead of on

69

the edge of the bench, while the snapping operation is carried out. It is worth trying this in case you find that you are happier with it.

Where only a very small portion is to be cut from a tile, the above method would not work, because it would be impossible to get sufficient leverage for a clean break. In these cases, mark the tile in the normal way then use an ordinary pair of pincers to snap the waste off bit by bit. Do not be over ambitious, however, and try to break off too much at a time with the pincers, or you will damage the tile. Minute amounts of tile can be filed off with an ordinary woodworking tool, but the hardness of the tile will, of course, soon blunt the file.

The above instructions refer to a cut that is made across the whole face of a tile. But sometimes rather more complicated cuts are needed. Perhaps the top corner has to be cut out to leave a tile that is roughly L-shaped. The tile must then be scored very carefully, with the spike, taking great care to ensure that the part of the tile you wish to retain will not be damaged. Then the shape is snipped out bit by bit with pincers. At other times it may be necessary to take out curved portions, to go round a bath or wash-basin, and, although this calls for a little more care in the original marking-out, the principles are the same. If a cut has to be made so that a tile can go round a water pipe, and this comes, as it inevitably will, in the centre of the tile, then the tile will have to be broken in two pieces, with the split coinciding with the centre of the pipe, and two equal half-round holes cut out in each half for the pipe.

Setting-out: This technique calls for time and patience, rather than a high degree of skill. By setting out, is meant arranging the tiles so that they fall neatly in position, and so that the half tiles at each end of a row are approximately equal. If you had an almost full tile at one end and a thin sliver of a tile at the other, it would look unsightly and unprofessional.

The items of equipment used in setting-out are a plumb-line and bob, a piece of timber of any convenient size to hold, and a few feet long, a ruler or tape measure, and a pencil. Measure the length of the wall and find the centre. From this point suspend the plumb-line, and mark its position on the wall with the pencil. Now set out a few tiles in a row on the floor, spacing them apart the correct distance for grouting. Put the length of timber alongside the tiles, and mark on the timber with the pencil the position of the tiles. Place this timber perfectly horizontal on the wall and use it to indicate where the tiles would fit in place. It may be preferable to start with a tile on each side of the plumb-line, or one placed centrally across it. Experiment with the timber until the tiles are well set out.

The skirting board: It is entirely a matter of personal preference whether or not you leave the skirting board in place in a fully tiled room. True, the professional usually removes it and carries the tiles right to the floor level, and thus gains a much better appearance. But the professional range of tiles has a much greater variety of shapes and accessories to offer and the craftsman may well fit specially curved tiles, or a coving, to neaten the join between floor and tiles. Such items would not be available in the thinner, do-it-yourself range of tiles. The amateur who felt that it was just not worth while, all things taken into consideration, to strip off the skirting board, would be well justified in his view.

Fixing the tiles: Floors, like walls, are not, in most houses, true, and this is especially so in a kitchen that may well have a floor of solid concrete, instead of sprung floorboards. If the skirting board has been removed, it will be necessary to fit a retaining batten, to stop the tiles sliding down the wall, as explained already under the heading of "Simple Tiling". This should be fixed one tile height up from the floor and a spirit level used to make sure that it is truly horizontal.

When the rest of the tiling has been completed, this batten can be removed, and the bottom row filled in, cutting the tiles as needed to meet any irregularities in the floor. Where the skirting board is to be left in place, it will serve the same purpose. It might be as well, though, to ensure that the skirting board is more or less horizontal. In a very old house it is possible that the walls and floor could be so far out of true that the lines of tiles placed at right angles to the skirting board would be obviously out of vertical. In this case, it would probably be best to get rid of the board and work from a batten you know to be horizontal.

Placing the tiles on the wall is now just the same as for the simple splashback, with the one proviso that if the adhesive is to be plastered on the wall, rather than the back of the tile, it would be as well not to put on more than you can reasonably cope with before it sets hard. Only experience could tell you exactly how much this would be. Place all the whole tiles in position first before you start to cut any. Tackle the grouting last of all.

Even in fully tiled rooms, ceramic tiles are never fixed to a ceiling. The ceiling should be treated with a paint, preferably chosen to tone in with the colour of the tiles. Or it can have tiles of expanded polystyrene, as explained below.

Polystyrene tiles: There are many reason why tiles of expanded polystyrene should be stuck on a ceiling. They help to combat condensation in kitchens and bathrooms, and where the condensation is only slight they might eliminate it almost entirely. They are also a means of increasing a room's insulation if the roof space above is not accessible for an insulating material to be laid there. If, incidentally, you want to test the insulating power of expanded polystyrene, place your hand on a tile. You will feel it immediately start to get warmer. Finally, these tiles offer a cheap and speedy way for the amateur to cover up a badly damaged ceiling.

Fixing the tiles: This is a very simple job, using one of the special adhesives, such as Polycell heavy duty, supplied for these tiles. Some manufacturers, incidentally, recommend that you "butter" the whole back of the tile with the adhesive; others merely suggest five spots of it, one at each corner and another in the middle. Always follow the recommendations of the manufacturers.

The tiles are merely offered up to the ceiling, slid into their exact position, pressed lightly home and left there for the glue to set. There is just one difficulty, and that is that you might, in pressing them in place, slightly dent the face, for the tiles are quite fragile. A simple tool will obviate this and it is well worth the while of anyone tiling a big area making it.

To make it, take a piece of plywood or blockboard, about ¾ or ½ in. thick, and the exact size of one of the tiles. Take a 1-ft. length of broomstick to act as a handle, and nail and glue this to the centre of the blockboard – you can bore a hole half-way through the board if you wish. Glue one of the tiles, with the bevelled side upwards to the board. Place a tile ready to be fixed to the ceiling on the board, offer it up, and lightly press it, without any fear of damaging it.

Setting-out: This is very important with ceiling tiles, for their bevelled edges create a distinct pattern of lines. If these are not true and orderly, they create a chaotic effect that looks most amateurish and unsightly. It is, therefore, vital that you put the first tile in exactly the right place, and then butt all subsequent ones fairly and squarely against each other. Then you should not go wrong.

Do not be tempted to start up against one side wall, especially in a corner. Apart from the fact that you cannot rely on the walls being true, the visual effect of whole tiles against one wall, and half ones – possibly even thin slices of tile – at the other, will be most displeasing. You must begin in the middle of the ceiling.

Take the two shortest walls in a rectangular room, or

any two facing each other in a square room, and measure them to find their exact centres. Mark these, and then snap a chalk line between them. For those readers unfamiliar with this phrase, it consists of driving home nails into the ceiling at the centre points, running a tight piece of string between them, rubbing chalk on the ceiling side of the string, pulling the string back as though it were on a bow, and letting it go twang against the ceiling. A firmly defined line will then be seen. It is, of course, necessary to choose a chalk that contrasts well with the colour of the ceiling. Measure along the chalk line and mark its exact centre. If the ceiling rose gets in the way of this line you can work one tile's width to the side of it.

You then need a length of wood a few feet long, as in the case of ceramic tiles. Put half a dozen or so tiles on the floor pushed hard up against each other, place the wood near the tiles, and mark their position on it. Place this wood on the ceiling, and determine whether you would get a better distribution of tiles by placing one on each side of the string line, or putting the first one centrally across it.

Once you have placed the first tile, or tiles, in place, it is merely a question of making sure that all the others are butted up hard against each other. Place all the whole tiles in position first, before you start to cut any half ones round the edges.

Cutting the tiles: This is very simple, and is best done with a sharp craft knife. Measure the gap at both ends, in case the wall is badly out of true, mark the tile with a pencil, place a straightedge across it, and draw the knife firmly across. Do not be tempted to use scissors on these tiles, for they will merely crush them instead of cutting cleanly.

If you have cut the tiles badly, and there is a ragged line all the way round the edges, you can neaten this by fixing there one of the coves made in polystyrene. These are handled, cut, and glued in place just like the tiles.

74

Household Heating

What is central heating?: Central heating is usually defined as meaning "a system of heating that utilizes the heat from one main source to warm some or all of the rest of the building". Thus this rules out many systems that are claimed to be central heating. These may offer whole house heating, but they do so by putting a separate heating appliance in every room. By the term *full* central heating, heating engineers usually mean a system that, when the temperature outside is on or about freezing point, will guarantee 65 to 70 degrees in the main living rooms, 55 degrees in the bedrooms, and 60 degrees in other parts of the house. The terms "partial central heating" and "background central heating" have no precise meaning, and anyone thinking of buying a central heating system should ask the seller exactly what he is offering.

Here are some of the things that have been offered as central heating: full comfortable heating when the weather is mild, but "topping up" necessary during really cold spells; heating confined to the main living rooms; a temperature of fifty degrees during freezing weather in the bedrooms, with living rooms heated by open fires; towel rails in bathroom and kitchen, plus an extra radiator in the hall, with no specific promises about what temperatures the system can guarantee. This is not to condemn the partial and background systems. Some of them offer excellent value, and may be just what the individual householder wants and what he can afford. We are merely stressing very strongly that anyone about to buy central heating should make sure what he is getting for his money, to avoid disappointments later on.

Types of central heating: When the layman thinks of central heating, he usually visualizes hot water circulating round pipes and radiators – what the technicians call the "wet" system – and this is indeed the most popular kind. The pipework now used in domestic situations is small bore – i.e. copper tubes that can be as little as $\frac{1}{2}$-in. in diameter in conjunction with slim, panel radiators. It is the substitution of these for the old large bore pipes and ugly column radiators that has, to a large extent, been responsible for the increasing popularity of central heating. For they are neat and unobtrusive, less expensive, and they can be installed with much less disturbance to the household. Thus a small bore wet system is ideally suited to installation in an existing house as well as to a newly built house.

The "dry" system of heating is one that distributes the warmth by blowing hot air along ducts and out through grilles into the various rooms of the house. It is a comparatively cheap system to install in a house while it is being built, but its installation in existing homes raises the problem of hiding the ducts, which are quite large and unsightly. Whether the problem can be overcome or not depends on the construction of the house. The installation is likely to be more successful in a large rambling old house, which perhaps has cellars and big rooms, than in a small, modern compact one.

The third kind of central heating is the electric storage system, in which electric heating elements warm up a solid mass – a concrete floor, or a pack of bricks in a metal container – and the heat is emitted as required.

These are usually off-peak systems that were devised to use up the surplus capacity of power stations, which are under-used during the night. The heat is poured into the solid mass during the night – with sometimes a midday boost – and is released during the day and evening. Where this takes the form of underfloor heating, it is obviously suited only to installation in a new house.

The hot water system: This is the system that most people will settle for. Water is heated in a boiler that can be fired by solid fuel, gas, or oil, and is then forced round the narrow pipes and slim radiators by an electric pump. As well as the small-bore flow and return pipes to the radiators, the system has a flow and return to the hot-water cylinder in the airing cupboard. These pipes will be large bore, because there is no pump, the system working by what is known as thermosyphonic action – which is the technician's way of saying that warm water rises, whilst cold water falls.

This cylinder will be what is termed an indirect cylinder – i.e. it consists of an inner and an outer cylinder. The pipes from the boiler are connected to the inner cylinder and they warm the water in this. As the outer casing of this inner cylinder heats up it warms the water in the outer cylinder, and it is this that is drawn off at the domestic taps. The whole point of this arrangement is to separate the water used at the taps from that which has swirled around the heating system, where it will have picked up rust and dirt.

Throughout in referring to this system, we have spoken of radiators, but these are not the only means of dis-charging heat into a room, and there is in fact a disad-vantage to radiators. Even the small modern kind have a certain bulk, and they take up valuable wall space where a householder might wish to put furniture. If they are placed under windows – a spot that most heating engineers recommend, because cold air is thus warmed up imme-diately it enters the room – they cannot be covered up by full-length curtains, which many housewives will prefer.

Instead of a radiator, it is possible for a convector heater to be installed – this, incidentally is an appliance for connecting up to a hot water central heating system, and should not be confused with a portable oil or electric convector. The point about these convectors is that they are fan-assisted, and the heat is forced out of them. They can thus be much smaller than a radiator, out of which the heat just drifts, as it were.

Another alternative is the skirting heater, and this is installed in place of a room's existing skirting board, which has to be taken out. A skirting heater consists of a pipe running all round the room, but covered in a decorative fashion by metal and/or wood, according to type. Various makes of heater offer different refinements in the way of grilles and openings that can be closed when the room is not in use. The main snag about skirting heaters is that you have to be sure there is enough wall to give a pipe run long enough to supply all the heat that a room needs.

Which is the best fuel?: This is an impossible question to answer, because there is no one fuel that is best in all situations. The only course is to study the pros and cons of each of them, and decide which best meets the needs of an individual case.

First, installation costs. Solid fuel is usually thought of as being the cheapest way to get a satisfactory heating system, and to a large extent this is true. In any installation the cost of the pipework and the radiators should be the same, and it is to the boiler that we have to look to discover any differences. Normally, a solid fuel boiler can be bought and installed cheaper than any other. This is especially so for the household that already has an old coke boiler in its kitchen. The new central heating boiler will take the place of this, and probably use exactly the same flue, to make for a comparatively cheap installation. Of course, if there is not already a boiler in the kitchen; if there is no room for the new boiler; if a special outhouse has to be built to accommodate it; if a flue has to be created from scratch – these are all complications that will affect the ultimate pricing. Each individual case has to be examined on its merits.

There are cases where a gas boiler can be bought and installed for less than a solid fuel boiler, but often it will cost more. If it takes the place of an old coke boiler, the existing flue needs a special lining to cope with the "exhaust" from the gas boiler, the boiler has to be connected up to the main, and most certainly a new, bigger gas meter will be called for, even if one already exists in the house.

An oil installation is normally the costliest of all. The boilers are, by and large, dearer, but it is the expense of the storage tank, which has to hold a lot of oil in safety, that really sends up installation costs.

Running costs: Secondly, running costs. It is here that we enter very difficult territory, and the recent geological discoveries round the British Isles may change the picture completely. But at present it is, broadly speaking, true to say that a given quantity of heat can be produced most cheaply of all by solid fuel, and more cheaply by oil than by gas. However, it is as well to bear in mind that the householder will be charged for his gas at a cheaper tariff, and this applies not only to the fuel used for the boiler, but also gas used for any other purpose, such as cooking, or summer water heating. The resultant cheaper water heating and cooking should be taken into account.

Controls: Anyway, the whole position is complicated by the next subject we have to consider, namely flexibility. Boilers can be controlled automatically in two ways, and the first of these is by time clock. A time clock can mean that the boiler is switched on automatically at the same time each morning – say, half an hour before the family rises – and off just after their normal bedtime at night. In addition, there can be two, and sometimes three, on-off operations so that for example, the boiler switches on just before the family rises, off as they all go out to work, on again at lunch time, then off again, and finally on to make sure the family returns to a warm house in the evening, finally switching off once again at bedtime.

The fact that systems can be shut off completely at night is the perfect answer to those who say they do not like central heating because it makes the bedrooms stuffy and they cannot sleep. It is also possible to have domestic hot water at a time when room heating is not required.

The other form of control is by thermostat, which can be used to control the temperature of the water in the boiler and, ultimately, in the radiators, and at the domestic tap. There can also be a wall thermostat, measuring the temperature in the main living room, and switching off the pump, thereby stopping the flow of heat to the radiators, when it gets too hot.

Some of these controls are quite rudimentary; others are incorporated into sophisticated control panels. Now it is obvious that gas and oil boilers are more suited to automatic control than are solid fuel ones. In fact, quite patently, it is impossible for a time switch or thermostat to put out a fire and re-light it in the same way that it can turn on and off a supply of gas or oil.

It remains true that oil and gas are more flexible than solid fuel, and if we are dealing with a grown-up family that spends a lot of time out of the house, the fact that boilers operated by these two fuels can be shut off completely and switched on easily by automation may well outweigh their extra running cost.

Fuel storage: Finally, we come to convenience, and here gas wins. There is no fuel to store, for it comes into the house by pipe straight from the works. There is no stoking of the boiler, for the gas is fed in directly as and when it is needed. There is no ash to empty, and no need to clean out the boiler periodically to re-light it. You do not have to keep a watch on the amount of fuel you have in store, in case you run out at a critical moment, because you can get as much as you want at the turn of a tap. And anyone with fears about safety, in view of memories of antiquated old gas fires in cheap hotels or bed-sitting rooms, can forget them – the modern gas boiler is adequately provided with all that is necessary in the way of automatic cut-outs.

Oil is not quite so flexible a fuel as gas, but it is almost so. There is the question of delivery of fuel, but the big oil companies have made this a painless business. However, the fuel needs to be delivered and stored, and this is something that has to be faced.

Coal is the least convenient of fuels. Nevertheless, the modern, highly efficient central heating boilers are a different race entirely from those old fashioned monsters of bitter memory, with which one battled every winter. Raking, cleaning, ash-clearing, stoking are nothing like the problem they used to be. But they are still chores that have to be faced, and they might put many people off. Once again, there is the problem of delivery and storage of fuel.

Whatever fuel is chosen, however, it is important that the system should be properly designed by a qualified person, and that advice should be sought from several firms and the suppliers of all types of fuel before a decision is reached. The correct size of radiator to give the desired standard of temperature in the room must be chosen. Then a boiler has to be selected capable of giving sufficient hot water to all the radiators, with some to spare for domestic purposes. Pipe runs must be designed so that the water will flow and return properly and so that some radiators are not starved of water, while the others get too hot. Finally, the right system of automatic controls should be worked out. It is failure to ensure a properly designed system that causes most of the complaints about central heating.

Hot air systems: Gas and oil are the usual fuels for these, although some solid fuel types do exist. This is how they work. Air is drawn through a grille from the various rooms served by the system, is passed over a heating unit – it would be incorrect to call this a boiler, because hot-water heating is not involved – and passed back into the room through a different grille. The advantages of this system are many. It is highly flexible and subject to very fine control by both time clock and thermostat, as described for the hot-water systems. The grilles are most unobtrusive, and do not cause the furnishing problems associated with radiators. There can be finger-tip control to shut off the grilles in various rooms, thus concentrating all the heat in one or more chosen rooms to get a very fast build-up. They can be installed very cheaply in new houses. Finally, you can use them to blow cold air throughout the house during a summer heatwave.

There are two big snags. Firstly, the ducts for the air are not neat and unobtrusive, like small-bore copper pipes. They are large and unsightly, and they need to be hidden. This is not a particularly difficult problem if the heating is installed during the actual construction of the house, but it can raise insuperable problems for anyone wishing to install ducted hot air in a house that is already built.

Secondly, since no hot water is involved, an entirely separate system of providing the domestic hot water must be provided.

Electric storage systems: The underlying thought behind these systems is that during the night, when very few domestic consumers are using electricity and even the industrial demand is nowhere near that in the daytime, there is a lot of spare power station capacity lying idle. The power stations cannot make electricity and store it, but it is possible for the power to be turned into heat which can be stored. Electric heating elements could be hidden in solid concrete or bricks and these would store the heat pumped into them during the night. By day the heat would be released to keep the home warm. The consumer's meter could be controlled by a sealed time switch that regulated the hours during which electricity was used.

There were obvious snags. The amount of heat pumped during the night could be controlled by thermostat, so that during a very cold night more heat would be stored to be released during the very cold day that would presumably follow. But in our notoriously unstable climate, who can say that a cold day will follow a cold night, or a warm day a warm night? So at first there were complaints that householders were having to open windows to release heat that they had paid for, or were shivering because not enough heat had been reserved for them during the night. Another point was that the heat gradually tailed off so that there was least of it when most was needed – during the late evening.

From these rudimentary beginnings, however, a whole new way of heating the small home has grown up, and the system has many, many satisfied customers.

The first domestic installations took the form of underfloor heating. The whole ground floor of a house was built of solid concrete with the heating cables bedded in it. On these floors some (but not all – it is always wise to check first) types of tile and parquet flooring could be fixed. The heat released all over the ground floor would, of course, rise to the upstairs floor, keeping this comfortably warm, too. This was, obviously a system suited only to installation while a house was being built.

Next came electric storage heaters, consisting of bricks with a metal and/or timber casing handsomely designed to fit in with modern furnishing schemes, and one of these was to be placed in every room. Later came more sophisticated versions of these with blowers, many of them thermostatically controlled, to boost the heat output during very cold weather. Now there are high-output, fully automated storage heaters that feed warm air into a duct system, which is designed to warm the whole house.

The arrangements for off-peak heating vary in different parts of the country, and even the same electricity board may well offer different rates for different periods of connection to the supply. Anyone thinking of having off-peak heating should discuss the matter thoroughly with his local electricity board. Do not plump straight away for the cheapest rates, because the period of charge may not be long enough, especially with the less sophisticated appliances. Many people, for instance, have found that it is worth while paying the extra to get a midday boost, if possible.

With electric storage heating, there is again the drawback that, since no hot water is involved, a separate system for domestic hot water is necessary.

When choosing the means of supplying this, bear one important principle in mind. If you are buying your fuel at a cheaper rate because you are getting bulk supplies – if, for instance, you are on a very cheap, two-part tariff for gas – it would be economical to use the same fuel for water heating. To mix fuels is a very expensive way of buying them. Obviously, anyone would be ill advised to heat a home by oil, cook by gas, and supply hot water by electricity.

Keeping the heat in: Fuel is so expensive that it is the height of folly to use it to create warmth in the home, and then let this heat escape into the cold night immediately. Yet that is what many families do. They simply throw their heat away. But not only does adequate insulation cut down on the running costs of a heating system; if it is done properly, it can also transform an under-powered heating system into one that is perfectly adequate.

Roofs: Since warm air rises, one of the most important escape routes for warmth is up through the ceiling, into the roof space, out through the roof and into the cold night. In a home that has an accessible roof space, insulation material can be laid down to prevent a lot of the heat from escaping. There are two basic kinds of insulating material – the sheet kind, and the loose-fill. The sheets can be made of aluminium foil, glass fibre or mineral wool. Aluminium foil is laid across the joists, and stapled to them, or crumpled slightly and pressed down between them. Blankets of glass fibre or mineral wool can be bought to a standard width that will fit neatly between the joists, or they can be laid across them like the foil. They do not, however, require any fixing, but they should be well tucked in at the eaves, to prevent any cold air blowing under them. In a very cold house, a double layer of blanket can be laid for extra insulation. Always wear gloves when handling glass fibre, since it can scratch the hands badly.

Unless a house is properly insulated, heat escapes and is replaced by cold air

Loose-fill materials are vermiculite granules and mineral wool pellets, which are merely poured between the joists. These have a slight self-adhesive quality so that they stick together and do not blow about the loft if there is a draught.

To be really weatherproof, a roof should have roofing felt, which is nailed across the rafters before the tiles are fixed in position. In many homes this was not done when the house was built, and, even if it was, the felt may since have deteriorated. Now is the time to renew it. Obviously it is not practical to strip off the tiles to place the felt in position, and at this stage the felt should be nailed to the inside of the rafters, or thin strips cut to go between them and fixed to them with thin laths.

When a loft has been properly insulated, it will be a much colder place. There is thus a chance that water tanks and pipes that have survived previous winters without frost trouble will now be in danger of freezing up. Therefore these should be properly insulated. Blankets can be merely thrown over the tank, or a box made to go round it and the box filled with loose-fill. Lagging should be wrapped round the pipes, or one of the clip-on insulators fixed to it. Insulating material should not be placed under the tank, and then warm air can still rise to keep the water in it above freezing point.

Not all loft spaces are accessible, of course. In the case of very modern houses this probably does not matter, because the chances are that it will have been insulated to a satisfactory standard. In older homes, however, this may not be the case, and the insulation will therefore have to be fixed to the ceiling. Probably the handiest way of doing this is to fix tiles of expanded polystyrene, or insulating fibre board, to the ceiling. In really bad cases, it might be necessary to create a false ceiling with insulating material packed above it. Battens of 2-in. sq. timber could be screwed through the plaster of the ceiling into the joists, and plasterboard, sheets of plywood, or lengths of timber if a timber décor were desired, fixed to these battens. Loose-fill should be rammed in the gap between the ceilings as the work proceeds.

Double glazing windows: Glass is a very poor insulator, and heat escapes through the windows of the home, particularly with the modern tendency to have the larger window areas, which make today's homes lighter and more cheerful. One obvious answer is to have good thick curtains, with a proper lining, and these will act as excellent insulators. It is possible, too, to buy curtain lining material made of a thin sheet of metal, and this increases even further the insulation value of curtains. Curtains should be considered not only for room windows, but also for such less obvious locations as the front and back doorways, especially if these have any glazing in them.

But curtains are not drawn all the time, of course, and there comes the problem of what to do during the hours of daylight. The best answer of all is proper double glazing, which will cut the heat loss by as much as a half. By proper double glazing we mean window panes that consist of two sheets of glass joined together with a gap between them of at most $\frac{3}{4}$ in., and hermetically sealed to eliminate condensation.

Double-glazing units are best fitted into frames specially designed to receive them and installed when the house is built. It is, however, possible to buy units that can be fitted into existing frames.

This type of double glazing is, however, far from cheap, and most households are looking for something less expensive. Whilst these, obviously, cannot be quite as effective as the proper thing, there is no doubt that they do have a most beneficial effect in reducing heat losses, stopping draughts, and reducing noise.

The most usual form they take is a kit, like the "Quick-Fix" Double Glazing System supplied by Messrs J. F. Finnegan & Co. Ltd., 847 Eccleshall Road, Sheffield 11. This kit consists of plastic beading that clips on to the existing window-frame and holds a second sheet of glass in place. With the aid of a special mitre guide tool the beading can be expertly cut at the corners so that the channelling fits right round the pane of glass. Swivel clips are screwed into the wooden frame at 12″ intervals which hold the channelling and glass securely in position but allow the pane to be easily removed or replaced at a moment's notice. In some cases the glass is not supplied as part of the kit, but has to be bought separately from your local builders' merchant. When properly assembled

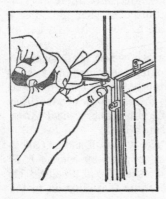

Quick-Fix is a simple and economical system for double glazing. These drawings illustrate the procedure for measuring and cutting the channel; fitting Quick-Fix to the glass; and tightening the clips in a frame of Quick-Fix

this double glazing has a most pleasing appearance at a fraction of the cost of a professionally installed system.

Choose a dry day, if possible, to install this type of double glazing, and first wash what will be the two interior glass surfaces with a household disinfectant, and polish them. The disinfectant will inhibit the risk of mould forming between the panes. If condensation does occur, the best way out is to drill a series of drainage holes in the lower window sill, so that any water will run away to the outside of the house.

Floors: There are seldom any draught problems with a solid floor, but over the years, tongued and grooved boards shrink, causing gaps through which cold currents of air shoot up. The problem is especially acute at ground floor level, where there is a space, and possibly a cellar underneath them. Any wall-to-wall flooring – carpets, parquet, cork or thermoplastic tiles – will cure the problem. If a flexible flooring is being put down – such as lino or plastic in sheet form – the gaps might cause ridges to show through. This will not happen if, first of all, sheets of standard $\frac{1}{8}$-in. hardboard are laid on the floor. The hardboard should be nailed at 6 in. centres to the floorboards. Gaps also develop between the floor and the skirting board. Quarter-round moulding nailed in place will cover these. Mitre the moulding at the corners.

Walls: The cavity walls of a modern house, which consist of two separate courses of brickwork with a gap in between them, are good insulators. Older houses, however, may have solid walls and these are not such good retainers of heat. In any event, there might be a north-facing wall, or one that is particularly exposed, and this could be permanently cold, dragging down the temperature of the rest of the room with it. It is worthwhile trying to do something about this. It is possible to buy expanded polystyrene – the material of which ceiling tiles are made – in sheet form, and paste it to the wall, underneath ordinary wallpaper. This has quite good insulation qualities.

Timber cladding is a popular form of interior decoration today, and this will be warmer than the cold plaster on the wall. It should be nailed to 2 × 1 in. battens screwed into wall-plugs. If insulating material – the sort used in the loft – is pushed behind it, the effect will be even more beneficial. People who do not like timber can still create a false wall by nailing sheets of hardboard or plywood to the battens, and applying a normal decorative finish to these.

Draught-proofing: This should not be carried out too thoroughly. Room heaters need a supply of air for combustion, and the draughts are caused as these appliances draw into the room more air to use. In fact, one of the many points in favour of central heating is that the individual radiators in each room do not need to create draughts to work efficiently. But open fires, gas fires and oil stoves do. If you shut off all the air entrances completely, they will not work properly. More important, human beings need a changing supply of air, too. It would be possible to seal off a room most effectively, but the result would be an unpleasant atmosphere.

Nevertheless, most homes certainly admit more draughts than are necessary, and perhaps a good compromise is to shut off all draughts coming through window and exterior door openings, but not to draught-proof interior doors.

The best way to go draught-hunting is with a lighted taper. Move it slowly round all exterior doors and window-frames. Note where its light flickers. These are the spots where action must be taken.

There are many proprietary draught-proofing aids available, and most of them are excellent. Before buying any, however, make sure they will do the job you are asking of them. Take note of how big a gap the material has to fill and ask the shopkeeper, or look on the back of the packet, to see if it is capable of filling such a space.

It often happens that a door or window has shrunk so much that no draught-proofer on the market can fill the resulting gap. In that case, the actual size of the door or window will have to be increased with a thin lath nailed in place.

The main forms of draught-proofing are self-adhesive foam strip, or sprung metal strip that is pinned in place. In addition there is a large range of draught-proofing kits for the foot of doors. There are many variations, but most of them work on the principle of a strip of rubber that springs up to seal the gap at the bottom of the door.

Curing condensation: Condensation results from the simple elementary law of physics that warm air will hold more moisture than cold air. In a kitchen, which is the top trouble spot for condensation in most homes, the cooker and household boiler warm up the air. There is a lot of moisture for this hot air to hold there. In addition to the natural air moisture, there is the vapour from boiling pans and kettles. Gas cookers also add water to the air as a by-product of combustion. This warm air then strikes a cold object – it may be the cold, hard surface of ceramic wall tiles, of gloss paint on doors or walls, of the kitchen window. Immediately as the air cools down it has to shed moisture. And this cascades down the walls and window causing what is commonly termed condensation.

There are two ways to get rid of it all. One is by improving ventilation, the other by improving the thermal insulation.

You cannot improve the ventilation merely by opening a window, because cold air will rush in, cool off the existing air in the room, and cause more condensation. The best way of getting rid of the saturated air is by extractor fan. True, this involves the householder in some expense. It is up to him to decide whether his condensation problem is bad enough to justify the outlay.

An extractor fan can be installed by the handyman, if there is a convenient electric socket nearby. He should place the fan as high as possible in the window or wall, and close to the sink and cooker if possible. But an extractor fan may affect the performance of a central heating boiler, so, if there is one of these in the kitchen, advice should be sought from the makers.

The aim of thermal insulation is to get rid of as many cold surfaces as possible, and some of the ways of doing so are similar to the insulation methods discussed above. For example, timber cladding, polystyrene sheets under wallpaper, double glazing for the window, a sleeve of polystyrene insulation for cold water pipes, draught-proofing round door- and window-frames to stop the entry of cold air. In addition a redecoration scheme could replace the gloss paint on the walls with one of the many versatile emulsion paints, and a flat paint could be used on the woodwork. Polystyrene tiles would keep the ceiling warm. An anti-condensation paint, which holds a certain amount of moisture on its surface and gradually releases it as the air becomes drier, could be put on the cold water pipes instead of the lagging.

Another bad spot for condensation is the bathroom. In fact, when a bath is being filled and near-boiling water is gushing out of the hot tap, the problem can be worse than in the kitchen. The remedies are similar, with the additional one that, if two separate bath taps can be replaced by one mixer unit during any scheme of bathroom modernization that is being carried out, then this will cut down on the amount of steam in the room, and thus reduce the condensation.

Basic Cookery

Measures: Most recipes are easy to follow, but interpreting measures into practical terms can offer problems. If you don't have a set of kitchen scales, here are some simple ways to work out weights with spoons. In each case, quantities are quoted for level spoonfuls.

For flour, cornflour, cocoa, custard-powder:
¼ oz. equals approx. 2 level teaspoonfuls or 1 level dessertspoonful
½ oz. equals approx. 2 level dessertspoonfuls or 1 level tablespoonful
1 oz. equals approx. 2 level tablespoonfuls

For sugar, rice, lentils:
1 oz. equals approx. 1 level tablespoonful

For breadcrumbs:
¼ oz. equals approx. 1 level tablespoonful

For syrup or treacle:
1½ oz. equals approx. 1 tablespoonful. And if you're wondering how to extract one spoonful without trailing the rest behind, warm the spoon first, and the treacle will come away cleanly.

For liquids:
The only really accurate method is to use a graduated

measure, or Pyrex jug with measures. But as a rough guide, it can be taken that a tea-cup holds one third of a pint. As tea-cup sizes vary, check with an empty milk bottle. Remember, it is difficult for recipes to give the exact amount of liquid required. Some flours absorb more moisture than others, and the size of an egg can vary, so learn to judge by experience how much is needed to get the correct consistency.

Meat: It can be cooked by almost any method, but the most popular methods are roasting, grilling, frying, stewing and braising. As a rough guide, roasting is best kept for large joints of good quality meat, grilling and frying for such things as steak and chops, and braising and stewing for poorer quality meats, which need long cooking to make them tender.

For roasting, weigh the joint and calculate the average cooking time as follows: for small joints of lamb or beef, allow 15 minutes per lb., plus 15 minutes; for thicker joints, allow 20–25 minutes per lb., plus 20–25 minutes. For veal and pork, allow 25–30 minutes per lb., plus 25–30 minutes, and never serve underdone.

To prepare joints for cooking, wash the meat in cold water. Trim off any excess fat then weigh the joint and calculate cooking time. Put the meat in a tin, and spread with lard, or dripping if available. Cook on the middle shelf of a moderately hot oven (400 degrees F., Gas Mark 6) for the first half-hour, and finish cooking at a slightly lower temperature (350 degrees F., Gas Mark 4). Baste with hot fat every 15–20 minutes to prevent the joint from becoming dry. For small joints that are liable to shrink, one should use a slower method of cooking. Place the meat in a cold oven, and raise the temperature quickly to 350 degrees F., Gas Mark 4. Continue cooking at this temperature throughout. Although the meat juices are not sealed by instant heat, as they are with the former method, the meat nevertheless remains moist and juicy. Whichever method proves most suitable, once the meat is cooked, certain juices will remain in the tin, from which gravy can be made. Pour off the excess fat, and put the tin over a low heat. Sprinkle in one teaspoonful of flour for beef, or two for lamb, mutton, veal or pork. Stir the flour into the fat until it is smooth and lightly browned. Then add gradually one pint of stock, or failing this, one pint of the liquid in which you cooked the accompanying vegetables. Stir over the heat until it is boiling, season to taste, and if desired, add a little gravy browning. Strain into a hot gravy boat.

For grilling, meats should be prepared as follows: steak should be cut 1–1½ in. thick, and should be beaten with a rolling pin to break down the fibres, thus making the meat more tender. Liver should be washed, dried, and cut into ½-in. slices. Kidneys should be washed, skinned and halved, and the cores should be removed. Chops should be trimmed neatly, and tied with string if a good shape is required.

Season all meats with salt and pepper, brush with oil or melted butter, and place on an oiled grid. The grill must be extremely hot to seal the surface and retain the juices, so it is essential that it is switched on two to three minutes beforehand. Always cook the meat for about two minutes on the first side, and then turn to the other side.

Turn frequently throughout, but avoid piercing the flesh, as the juices will escape. Steak that is 1½ in. thick takes 12–15 minutes to cook, but this varies according to taste.

Lamb chops take 8–10 minutes; pork chops 15–20 minutes; liver and kidneys 10 minutes; and sausages 15–20 minutes. Any meat that is suitable for grilling is also suitable for frying. It should be prepared in the same way, except that liver and kidneys may be rolled in seasoned flour before cooking, if desired. Heat fat in a frying pan, and cook the meat quickly on both sides to seal the juices. Then lower the heat and cook more gently, turning the meat from time to time. Cooking times will be about the same as for grilling.

Stewing means cooking meat in either stock or water, in

a covered saucepan on top of the stove, or in a casserole inside the oven. It provides an ideal method of dealing with the cheaper cuts of meat, where slow cooking makes the coarse fibres tender. Vegetables are usually added, and as all the liquid is used, none of the flavour or nourishment is wasted. There are two kinds of stew – white and brown. Mutton, veal and rabbit are suitable for the former, and no preliminary frying, or thickening of the liquid, is necessary.

Irish stew is a typical example of a white stew, and requires the following ingredients:

1 lb. middle neck of mutton; 2 large onions; 2 lb. potatoes; salt and pepper.

To prepare, wipe the mutton thoroughly, remove the spinal cord, and cut the meat into neat joints. Cut the onions and potatoes into rings, and make alternate layers of meat and vegetables in a large saucepan, sprinkling each layer with salt and pepper. Half-cover with water, bring to the boil, and simmer gently for about 1½ hours.

Stewing steak and oxtail are suitable for brown stews. Here is a recipe using stewing steak:

¾–1 lb. stewing steak; 1 onion; 2–3 carrots; ½ turnip; 1

stick celery; dripping; 1 oz. flour; 1 pint stock or water; seasoning; bouquet garni.

To prepare, wipe the meat and cut into neat pieces. Prepare the vegetables and dice or cut into rings. Melt the dripping in a large saucepan, and fry the vegetables until golden brown, then turn them out on to a plate. Brown the meat quickly on all sides in the dripping in the pan, and add to the vegetables.

Fry the flour in the remaining fat, adding a little more if needed, and stir constantly, until it turns a rich brown. Return the meat and vegetables to the saucepan, add the liquid, seasoning, and bouquet garni, and simmer for 2–4 hours. Alternatively, turn the contents of the saucepan into a casserole, and bake for about three hours in a moderate oven (325 degrees F., Gas Mark 3).

Braising is a combination of stewing, steaming and roasting, and is suitable for almost all meats. Slow cooking over a bed of vegetables results in a moist texture and delicate flavour.

Prepare the meat, wiping and trimming off any fat, and weigh to calculate the cooking time. Allow 20–25 minutes to the lb., plus 30 minutes. Prepare whichever vegetables you require – 1 onion, 1 carrot, 1 small turnip, 1 stick of celery – makes a good bed of vegetables. Fry them in about 1 oz. of dripping, plus a few bacon rinds, making sure there are enough to cover the bottom of the casserole well. Add a bouquet garni, and enough stock or water to three-quarters cover the vegetables. Bring to the boil, and place the meat on top. Cover the casserole, and cook for half the cooking time, in a slow to moderate oven (325–350 degrees F., Gas Mark 3–4), basting the meat with the liquid every 20 minutes. For the last half-hour, remove the lid and increase the temperature to hot (400 degrees F., Gas Mark 6), thus giving the meat the flavour of a roast. Before serving, remove the bouquet garni and the bacon rinds.

An alternative method of braising is to coat the meat with well-seasoned flour, and fry quickly in smoking hot dripping until brown all over. Remove from the pan, and fry the vegetables until lightly browned. Put the vegetables in the casserole plus a bouquet garni, place the meat on top, and add enough stock or water to cover just the vegetables. Cover, and cook in a slow to moderate oven (325–350 degrees F., Gas Mark 3–4), about 2–3 hours for stewing meat, 1–2 hours for rabbit, or 1 hour for chicken.

Vegetables: These should be used as soon as possible, especially green vegetables, and if they have to be stored, should be kept in a cool, airy place. Prepare them immediately prior to cooking, and avoid leaving them to soak.

For boiling, use as little water as possible, and add half a small teaspoonful of salt to each half-pint of water. Bring the water to the boil as quickly as possible. Cook with the lid on, for anything from 10 minutes for young green vegetables to 1 hour or more for undiced root vegetables. Potatoes take about 20 minutes, and this is about average.

Boiling is suitable for most vegetables, but some people prefer steaming, especially for root vegetables. This method, where the vegetables do not actually come into contact with the water, but are cooked in a container placed over rapidly boiling water, takes about half as long again as for boiling.

Baking is most popularly reserved for roast potatoes. The peeled, raw potatoes are seasoned, and placed around roasting meat for about an hour, being turned to ensure an even crispness.

Vegetable marrow, parsnips, carrots and Jerusalem artichokes are also delicious baked, and take about the same time to cook as potatoes, provided they, like the potatoes, are cut into even-sized pieces. If meat is not being roasted, vegetables can still be baked by placing them in a tin with a little dripping, and cooking in a moderately hot oven (400 degrees F., Gas Mark 6). Most root vegetables, onions, leeks and celery can be braised, follow the braising method as described above for meat.

The evaporation method of cooking vegetables has much to recommend it, for although it takes longer, the liquor that remains after cooking can be served, and retains the full flavour and nourishment. Carrots, turnips, celery and onions are best suited to this method, and should be prepared in the usual way, being left whole if young, and diced if old. Place them in a thick-bottomed saucepan, with a very little water, salt, pepper, and a knob of butter. Cover and cook, either in a slow oven (315 degrees F., Gas Mark 2), or over a low heat, until tender. This will take about 20–30 minutes for young vegetables, and anything from 1 to 1½ hours for old. Add more liquid if necessary, but no more than 1 to 2 tablespoons of liquid should remain at the end of cooking.

Soups: Most soups are improved if bone or vegetable stock is used instead of water. To make bone stock: put 2 lb. of uncooked mutton or lamb bones in a large saucepan, with pieces of vegetable such as carrot, onion and celery. Add a bunch of herbs and 1 teaspoon of salt. Cover with cold water, bring to the boil and simmer with the lid on for 2–3 hours. Strain, allow the stock to become cold, and skim off any fat. Bone stock should not be kept for more than three or four days, and should be boiled up daily. To make vegetable stock: use a variety of vegetables, such as carrots, celery, leeks etc., but avoid a large quantity of strongly-flavoured vegetables such as turnip, which would overpower the rest. Add a mixture of herbs, and a few bacon rinds if desired. Cover with water, and gently simmer with the lid on until a good mellow flavour is obtained. Strain. Always use while fresh.

Soups divide into two categories: thin (sub-divided into consommés and broths) and thick (sub-divided into purées and thickened soups). We give one example of each kind.

Plain Consommé

½ lb. lean beef; 1 small carrot; 1 small onion; piece of turnip; small stick of celery; 2 quarts bone stock or water; bouquet garni; a blade of mace; 12 peppercorns; 2 cloves; the whites and shells of 2 eggs; salt to taste; little sherry.

Shred the meat finely, and soak for about half an hour in just enough cold water to cover it. Prepare the vegetables, and cut each one into four. Put the stock, from which all traces of fat have been removed, into a large saucepan. Add the meat, and the water in which it has been soaked, the vegetables, herbs and spices. Lastly add the egg-whites and crushed egg-shells to clarify the soup and make it transparent. Bring nearly to boiling point, whisking all the time. Then stop whisking, and allow the froth to rise to the top of the saucepan. Draw away from the heat, but keep in a warm place for 5 minutes. Strain the consommé through scalded muslin into a basin, and repeat if not clear, using a fresh basin. Re-heat the consommé in the saucepan, adding salt if necessary, and also a little sherry, but add nothing that will make the soup cloudy.

Scotch Broth

1½–2 lb. lean beef; 2 quarts water; salt and pepper; 1 medium carrot; small turnip; 1 onion; 2 leeks; 1½ oz. pearl barley; 1 dessertspoon chopped parsley.

Put the meat, water and the seasoning into a saucepan, bring slowly to the boil, and simmer gently for 1½ hours. Add vegetables, all diced, and barley. (To prevent the broth from becoming cloudy, first blanch the barley, i.e. put the grain into cold water, bring to boiling point, and strain.) Continue to simmer for about 1 hour – until the barley and vegetables are cooked. Remove any fat, either with a spoon, or by passing absorbent kitchen paper over the surface. Serve meat separately if desired, with a little of the broth. Put chopped parsley into a tureen, and pour in the rest of the broth.

Cream of Tomato Soup

1 lb. tomatoes; 1 onion; 1 carrot; 1 stick celery; little fat bacon or bacon rinds; 1½ pints vegetable stock or water; salt and pepper; bouquet garni; 1 oz. flour or ¾ oz. cornflour; ½–¾ pint milk; pinch of sugar; chopped parsley or watercress.

Prepare and slice the tomatoes and other vegetables. Fry the bacon or rinds slowly to extract the fat. Add the vegetables, and sauté for about 10 minutes. Add the stock or water, seasoning and bouquet garni. Bring to the boil and simmer 1 hour – or until tender. Remove the bacon rinds and bouquet garni. Rub the soup through a fine sieve. Blend the flour or cornflour to a smooth cream with the milk, and add to the sieved soup. Return to the saucepan, bring to the boil, stirring well, and allow to boil for 2–3 minutes. Add the sugar, more salt and pepper if desired, and just before serving, add the chopped parsley or watercress.

Thick Oxtail Soup

1 oxtail; 2 onions; 1 carrot; 2 sticks of celery; 1 oz. butter or dripping; 3–4 pints bone or vegetable stock, or water; 1 oz. lean bacon or ham; bouquet garni; 1 bay leaf; 2 cloves; 6 peppercorns; salt and pepper; 1 oz. flour; little port wine (optional); squeeze of lemon juice.

Wash the oxtail, joint it, and dry the joints. Prepare and cut up the vegetables. Melt the fat in a large saucepan, and sauté the jointed oxtail and vegetables for a few minutes. Cover well with stock or water, and bring to the boil. Add the bacon or ham, herbs and seasoning. Put on the lid and simmer gently for about 4 hours, or until the meat is tender, skimming occasionally. Strain the soup. Remove the meat from the joints, cut up, and return to the strained soup. Replace in the saucepan, and stir in the flour, blended to a smooth cream with a little port wine or water. Bring to the boil stirring, and cook for about 5 minutes. Finally, add a squeeze of lemon juice, and more seasoning if desired.

All soups look more exciting with the addition of a garnish, which should be sprinkled over the surface immediately prior to serving. Toast croutons are simple to make, and are suitable for almost all soups. Toast white bread, remove the crusts, and cut into ¾-in. squares. Alternatively, cut slices of white bread into fancy shapes, and fry them in hot fat until crisp and golden brown. Serve grated Parmesan or Cheddar cheese with potato, leek or onion soups. Sprinkle 1½-in. bread squares with grated Parmesan, and float on French onion soup. Sliced cooked carrots can be cut into fancy shapes to serve with clear soups.

Bread and pastry: Home-baked bread is something we rarely have nowadays. It is well worth the trouble of learning how to bake it.

White Bread

Enough for 2 large, or 4 small loaves: 3½ lb. plain white flour; ½ oz. salt; 1 oz. fresh yeast, or ½ oz. dried yeast; 1 teaspoon caster sugar; approx. 1¾ pints tepid water.

Unless you want a tin loaf, you don't need any special utensils, as you can cook bread on an ordinary baking tray. Only unusual requirement: keep both utensils and ingredients warm, so that the yeast, which is a living plant, can grow.

Start by sieving warm flour and salt into a warmed bowl. If using fresh yeast, cream it with sugar; if using dried, follow instructions on packet – this usually means sprinkling the dried yeast and sugar into half a cup of tepid water, then leaving in a warm place until mixture has frothed to top of cup. Make a well in the flour, and pour in yeast mixture. Sprinkle flour lightly over the yeast liquid, and stand covered with a clean dish towel in a warm place.

After 20 mins., mix the dough, adding enough tepid water to make a smooth dough that leaves the sides of the bowl cleanly. Knead well until the mixture is smooth and elastic. Cover, and stand in a warm place again. After about 1 hour, the dough should have risen to double its size. Re-knead and cut into pieces, shaping each piece and kneading until free from cracks. Put into warm greased and floured baking tins, half filling them, or on to a warm greased and floured baking tray. Leave covered for 20–30 mins. in a warm place, until the mixture has doubled its size again. Put into a hot oven (425 degrees F., Gas Mark 7) for 15 mins., then reduce to moderate (350 degrees F., Gas Mark 4) and cook for about 25 mins. until the bread has risen and turned golden. To check if it is done, tap underside of loaves with the knuckles: they should sound hollow.

Wholemeal bread. Don't sieve, but just add 1 oz. of salt to 3 lb. of wholemeal flour. Rub in 2 oz. lard and leave bowl in warm place. Cream 1 oz. yeast with 2 teaspoons of sugar before adding half of 1¾ pints of tepid water. Make a well in the flour, add the yeast liquid, plus enough of the remaining liquid to make a fairly soft dough. You may find you need extra water. Knead thoroughly, and put to rise until double its size. Then continue as for white bread, except that wholemeal takes longer to bake (about 45–50 mins. in all for a large loaf).

For all kinds of bread, buy moist, compressed yeast from your baker or grocer. Use immediately, or if it has to be kept a few days, keep covered in a refrigerator.

Dried bakers' yeast is a useful standby and gives excellent results, but follow instructions on the tin carefully, as each make differs.

Pastry. Forget everything about bread-making and do the opposite. Keep ingredients and utensils cool. Handle the dough as little as possible, and don't knead it, or you'll get a tough and leathery result. Always roll in the same direction: turn the pastry round rather than altering the angle of the rolling-pin.

Rough puff pastry

8 oz. self-raising flour; pinch of salt; 6 oz. lard and margarine, mixed; cold water to mix.

This recipe will provide enough for one big covered pie. Sieve flour and salt into a bowl. Cut the fat into walnut-size pieces and drop into the flour. Add enough water to make a stiff dough, mixing it in with a knife. Turn on to a floured board, and roll into an oblong with a well-floured rolling-pin. Fold up the bottom third of your oblong, and fold down the top third, lightly pressing open edges together with the rolling-pin to trap in the air. Turn the pastry round so the fold is on the right. Roll the pastry to an oblong again, and repeat the process three or four times more, until the fat is thoroughly incorporated with the flour. Ideally, leave in a cool place for one hour –

or overnight if this is convenient. Roll to desired size and thickness, and bake for 15 mins. in a hot oven (450 degrees F., Gas Mark 8) for small items like tarts; for larger items, lower to moderately hot after 10 mins. (400 degrees F., Gas Mark 6) and continue baking for 20–30 mins.

Shortcrust pastry. You need the same ingredients, but only 4 oz. of fat. Sieve the flour and salt lightly into a bowl. Cut the fat into small pieces and add all at once. Rub the fat lightly into the flour with *fingertips only*, until no lumps remain visible, and the mixture becomes breadcrumb fine. Add cold water, a little at a time, and mix in with a knife; for the last stage of mixing use the fingers. The dough should be smooth and firm and leave the sides of the bowl cleanly. Place on a floured board, and again roll to the desired thickness and size. Bake as for rough puff pastry.

Cakes: You can choose from three basic categories: plain, rich and sponge. This is according to the proportion of fat, sugar and eggs they contain, and the method of making. Plain cakes need up to one half fat and sugar to flour, and are made by the rubbing-in method.

Plain Fruit Cake
8 oz. self-raising flour; pinch of salt; 3 oz. butter or margarine; 3 oz. sugar; 3–4 oz. dried fruit; 2 eggs; milk or water to mix.

Sieve the flour and salt. Rub fat in lightly with the fingertips, until the mixture looks like fine breadcrumbs. Add sugar and fruit. Beat the eggs and add, plus a little milk or water, mixing in quickly with a wooden spoon. Add more liquid if necessary to get a stiff dropping consistency (i.e. when the mixture takes about 4 seconds to drop unaided from the spoon). Grease a 6 in. cake tin, and fill three-quarters full. Bake in a moderate oven (350 degrees F., Gas Mark 4) for about 1 hour. Variations on the plain cake theme include farmhouse and rock cakes.

Rich Fruit Cake

6 oz. butter or margarine; 6 oz. sugar; 2–3 eggs; 8 oz. self-raising flour; 4 oz. dried mixed fruit; milk to mix.

Rich cakes contain higher proportions of fat and sugar, and are made by the creaming method.

Cream fat and sugar together in a large bowl, using the back of a wooden spoon. If the fat is hard, you can warm it slightly, but never let it get oily. Carry on creaming till the ingredients actually look like cream. Add the eggs gradually (if you add them all at once, the mixture will curdle) and beat vigorously, keeping the mixture smooth and creamy. Then fold in the sieved flour with a metal spoon, never beating. Add the fruit, and a little milk if necessary to get a soft dropping consistency. Grease a 7 in. cake tin and fill three-quarters full. Place in a moderate oven (350 degrees F., Gas Mark 4) for about 1 hour. Variations on the rich cake theme include Christmas and Madeira cake.

Sponge Cake

4 eggs; 6 oz. caster sugar; 4 oz. self-raising flour.

Sponge cakes usually contain no fat, but a high proportion of sugar and eggs, and are made by the whisking method.

Put the eggs and sugar into a large bowl, and place over a gentle heat. Begin to whisk immediately, until the mixture becomes thick, fluffy and stiff enough to keep the imprint of the whisk for a few seconds. This stage can take up to 15–20 mins., but the lightness of the cake depends largely upon it. Remove mixture from heat, and sift in one-third of the flour. Fold the flour in with a metal spoon, never beating, as this breaks the air bubbles already beaten in. Add the remaining flour in the same way, and pour the mixture into a greased, floured and sugar-dusted baking tin. Fill it three-quarters full, and bake in a moderate oven (350 degrees F., Gas Mark 4), for about one hour. Variations on this theme are chocolate log and Swiss roll.

Testing. To test that all kinds of cake are thoroughly cooked, insert a knife into the centre: it should come out clean and unsmeared.

Batters: The same basic batter recipe will serve for Yorkshire pudding, for savoury batters, pancakes and fritters.

For a Yorkshire pudding for 2–3 people, the following ingredients are required:

4 oz. self-raising flour; ½ teaspoon salt; 1 egg; ½ pint of milk or milk and water.

Sieve the flour and salt into a bowl, and make a well in the centre. Add the egg, and work into the dry ingredients gradually to avoid lumps. Keeping the mixture as smooth as possible, add about half the milk or milk and water. Tilt the bowl, and beat the liquid from side to side with a wooden spoon. When the mixture is smooth, add remaining liquid, and continue beating for 5 to 10 minutes. How well one beats the batter determines the number of air bubbles that are incorporated, and the amount the pudding will rise. The batter can be left to stand before using, and some people claim it is improved by so doing. Put a little dripping into a deep tin, and make this smoking hot in the oven. Pour in the batter, and bake in a hot oven (450 degrees F., Gas Mark 8) for 30–35 minutes.

For toad-in-the-hole, make the batter in precisely the same way, but add 1 lb. of sausages to the batter in the tin, and bake at the same temperature, for three-quarters to 1 hour; serve immediately.

For pancakes, again make the identical batter. Melt enough lard in a thick frying pan to coat bottom and sides, and pour off any surplus. When the fat is smoking hot, pour in sufficient batter to cover the bottom of the pan. Cook the pancake until it is golden-brown on the underside, toss, or if you feel cowardly, use a spatula to turn the pancake over and cook the second side. Fill with sweet or savoury contents, roll up the pancake, and serve at once. The traditional way to serve pancakes is to sprinkle them with sugar and lemon before rolling up.

For a coating batter, suitable for coating fish to be fried, or for making apple fritters, mix the same standard batter, but use only half the quantity of milk or milk and water.

For apple fritters, prepare and cut the fruit into rings. Coat each ring with batter, and let it drain. Heat enough fat in a thick frying pan to submerge the fritters, until a blue haze rises. Cook the fritters until they are golden-brown, turning them over as required. Drain well on absorbent paper, and serve sprinkled with sugar. Savoury fritters, with fillings such as prawns or corned beef, are made in the same way, but the batter mixture should be seasoned well with pepper and extra salt, and finely chopped onion can be added if required.

Jams: Home-made bread and pastry deserve home-made jam. There's no mystery to making it: if you boil fruit and sugar together – in the right proportions of course – you get jam. Jam sets because of pectin, a substance which is released by the sugar and fruit-acid in boiling. Fruits like cooking apples, damsons, gooseberries, and black currants are rich in pectin and acid. Apricots, plums, greengages, loganberries and raspberries, have them in sufficient quantities for setting. But strawberries, cherries and pears are poor in pectin and acid, and need the addition of lemon juice to help the jell.

Ideally, use a preserving pan, but otherwise a saucepan will do, provided it has a thick bottom so that the jam doesn't stick and burn. And only half fill a saucepan, or the jam may bubble over as it boils. First stage is to cook the fruit, which must be sound and just ripe. Simmer until it becomes soft, in the minimum amount of water possible. Definitely do not boil. For fruit poor in pectin, add the juice of one lemon for each pound, before simmering begins.

Once the fruit has cooked, add one pound of sugar (preferably preserving, otherwise granulated) to each pound of fruit. Stir until dissolved, and bring to the boil quickly. Start testing for a jell after about 5 minutes of boiling time – but it may take 10 or 15 minutes boiling before the jell is ready. Test by placing a teaspoonful of jam on a cold saucer, and leaving it to cool. If a skin forms that wrinkles when a finger is drawn across the surface the jam is ready. If there is no skin, continue boiling – and testing. Once ready, take off the hotplate immediately, and remove any scum that may have formed. Pour into warm, dry jars (old jam jars are the obvious choice), and cover immediately with waxed paper circles. While the jam is still hot, cover with circles of Cellophane, and secure with a rubber band. Store in a cool, dry, and if possible, dark place.

Bottling fruit: The easiest and most effective method of bottling fruit is the oven method, and this is suitable for all fruits – apples, pears, plums, cherries, raspberries, black currants etc., provided the fruit is ripe and reasonably firm.

Either water or syrup can be used, but syrup – made by boiling sugar in water, allowing about 8 oz. sugar to every pint of water – gives the fruit more flavour.

There are various types of jars available which are

suitable for bottling, but Kilner jars are one of the easiest and most convenient to use.

Begin by preparing the fruit carefully – wash it well, peel if necessary, then chop or slice, and pack tightly into the clean jars. When the jars are all filled, cover each with an old clean tin lid, stand them either on an asbestos mat or a wooden board, and put them into a cool oven (240 degrees F., Gas Mark ½) for about 1 hour – allow less time for soft fruits, such as raspberries and black currants; more for peaches and pears.

Take the jars out of the oven carefully, and quickly

pour boiling water or syrup into each jar until it overflows. At once seal with the rubber rings, and screw down lids. Leave jars in a cool place for 24 hours. Test lids to see if they have sealed properly – if they haven't, contents should be used at once. If they have sealed, then the fruit should keep for many months.

Cold drinks for hot days: On a hot summer day, what could be more refreshing than a jug of delicious, home-made lemonade? Fruit squashes and cordials are very easy and inexpensive to make – here are a few recipes to try.

Lemon squash
2 lemons; 4 oz. sugar; 1 pint boiling water.

110

Orange squash

2 oranges; 1 lemon; 1 oz. sugar; 1 pint boiling water.

Wash the fruit, wipe dry, and peel thinly. Put the peel and sugar into a jug, and pour on the boiling water. Cover, and allow to stand until cool, stirring occasionally. Add the juice of the peeled fruit, and strain before serving.

An alternative method is to wash and peel the fruit thinly. Put the peel, sugar, and half the water into a saucepan. Boil gently for about 10 minutes, and strain through muslin into a jug. When cold, add the rest of the water, and the strained juice of the fruit.

Lemonade (First method)

Juice of 2 lemons; sugar to taste; soda water.

Orangeade (First method)

Juice of 2 oranges; juice of 1 lemon; sugar to taste; soda water.

Put the strained fruit juice and sugar into a jug, and fill up with soda water.

Lemonade (Second method)

6 lemons; $\frac{1}{2}$ lb. sugar (or more to taste); $\frac{1}{2}$ pint water; 1 egg-white; ice cubes (optional); 1 siphon soda water.

Orangeade (Second method)

5 oranges; 1 lemon; $\frac{1}{4}$ lb. sugar; $\frac{1}{4}$ pint water; 1 egg-white; ice cubes (optional); 1 siphon soda water.

Peel thinly the rinds of two lemons for lemonade, or one orange and the lemon for orangeade. Put into a saucepan with the sugar and water, and boil gently for 10 minutes. Strain into a jug and allow to cool. Just before serving, add the strained fruit juices, the stiffly beaten egg-white, a few cubes of ice if desired, and finally the soda water.

Lemonade (Third method) Where the juice of several

lemons has been used in cooking, rather than waste the peel, it can be utilised for lemonade as follows:

Peel of 6 lemons; 1½ tablespoons Demerara sugar; 1 heaped teaspoon citric acid; 1 pint boiling water.

Put the thin peelings into a jug. Add the sugar and acid, and pour on the boiling water. Cover, and leave till it cools. Stir occasionally. Strain and serve.

Grapefruit Barley Water. This takes longer to make, but provides one of the most refreshing drinks of all.

2 oz. pearl barley; juice of 1 grapefruit; sugar to taste.

Wash the barley, cover with cold water in a saucepan, and bring to the boil. Strain and rinse the barley. Add 1½ pints of cold water, and boil slowly with the lid on for 1½–2 hours. Strain into a jug, and when cold, add grapefruit juice and sugar.

Drinks

It is usual to offer guests an aperitif on arrival. This aperitif has two purposes: it serves to stimulate the appetite and prepare the palate for the meal to follow, and it helps the conversation to get started, especially if you have guests who do not know each other too well.

Gin: This is the most English of all drinks, the great English contribution to the pleasures of the drinking world. It is to England what whisky is to Scotland, vodka to Russia, sherry to Spain, and port to Portugal. Gin is made in other countries too: and the Netherlands provide another popular variety called "Hollands". Nowadays, gin is the most popular pre-dinner drink in British homes, served mixed with tonic water, and sometimes with bitter lemon. Two other variations are Gin and It and Gin and French – meaning gin mixed with Italian and French Vermouth respectively. To all these drinks a cube of ice and a slice of lemon peel (except in the case of bitter lemon) is usually added.

Whisky: To people in Great Britain the word "whisky" is usually associated with Scotland, although Irish whiskey, (usually spelled with an "e") is popular. Scotch and Irish whiskies are both primarily made from barley. The

"Scotch" normally sold in England is a blend of malted and unmalted whiskies. But many English people have now come across that supreme delight, the unblended malt whisky, which seems an entirely different drink from the "Scotch" they are normally accustomed to.

The Americans make two sorts of whisky: Rye, distilled, naturally enough, from rye, and Bourbon, distilled from corn. The Canadians, too, make a rye whisky. Whisky is usually mixed with soda-water or dry ginger, although since the war the American habit of drinking it "on the rocks" – i.e. straight whisky poured over ice – has become popular.

Sherry: Considered by many to be the greatest of all predinner drinks. Sherry is a Spanish wine that comes from Jerez de la Frontera – and its name is a result of an English corruption of the name. Sherry comes in styles to suit all palates, dry, medium dry, medium sweet and sweet. "Sherries" from countries other than Spain – Australia, South Africa and the United States (California) – are available, but these must always be described by the name of their country of origin, such as "Australian Sherry."

Aperitifs: A whole series of aromatised wines – wines made from grapes in the normal way, then with herbs added – exist, and these make excellent pre-dinner drinks. Most famous is vermouth, of which there are two main types – French and Italian. The French is usually thought of as being lighter and drier (the famous dry Martini) while the Italian is red and sweeter. The Italians, however, do a famous white vermouth (bianco) which is sweet like the red ones, and there is another French variety called Chambéry. Vermouth can be served neat, or diluted with soda-water, with ice cubes and a slice of lemon added. Other popular wine aperitifs include St. Raphael and Dubonnet while bitters, such as Campari, are drunk neat, or mixed with gin.

Cocktails: A cocktail is a mixed drink usually with a base of gin, whisky, vodka or rum – to which various other ingredients are added. Some cocktails are mixed by shaking in a cocktail shaker, others are merely stirred. Here are recipes for some of the more popular cocktails.

Champagne Cocktail
  Chilled champagne; Angostura bitters; cube sugar; slice of orange.
  Put one cube of sugar in each glass. Add a dash of Angostura. Fill glass with champagne. Add slice of orange.

White Lady
  2 parts gin; 1 part Cointreau; 1 part lemon juice.
  Shake well with cracked ice, and strain before serving.

Manhattan
  2 parts whisky; 1 part French vermouth; dash of Angostura bitters; dash of Curaçao.
  Mix well and decorate each glass with a maraschino cherry.

Sidecar
  2 parts of brandy; 1 part gin; lemon.
  Mix all ingredients, adding juice of $\frac{1}{4}$ lemon for each glass, shake well with ice, and strain into glasses.

Dry Martini

2 parts gin; 1 part French vermouth; curl of lemon peel or green olive.

Add vermouth to ice cubes in a jug, add gin, stir well, strain and serve.

Whisky Sour

1 measure whisky; 1 teaspoon sugar; lemon.

For one person: mix whisky, sugar and the rind and juice of ¼ lemon with some crushed ice. Shake and strain.

Americano

1 part Campari; 1 part Italian red vermouth; curl of lemon rind.

Mix the ingredients in a tumbler with ice, add soda-water to taste.

Collins

1 measure of vodka or gin; 1 dessertspoon sugar; juice of ½ lemon; soda-water.

Put some ice in a tumbler, add vodka, sugar and lemon, mix and lastly add soda-water.

Negroni

1 part gin; 1 part Campari; 1 part Italian red vermouth; slice of orange; soda-water.

Put ice in a tall glass, add other ingredients, and mix – add the soda-water last.

Bacardi Dry

1 part Bacardi rum; 1 part French vermouth.

Stir together in a jug with plenty of ice. Strain and serve.

Gimlet

3 parts gin; soda-water; 1 part lemon juice.

Mix with ice, top up with soda-water.

Snowball

1 measure Advocaat; lime juice; lemonade.

Mix Advocaat with a dash of lime juice. Add lemonade to taste. Decorate with a cherry.

Black Velvet
1 part champagne; 1 part stout.
   Using a tall tumbler – pour gently

Maiden's Prayer
3 parts gin; 3 parts cointreau; 1 part lemon juice; 1 part orange juice.
   Shake with cracked ice. Strain and serve.

Old Fashioned
1 measure Bourbon whisky; Angostura bitters; sugar; soda-water.
   Crush a lump of sugar in a medium-sized tumbler, add Angostura, mix. Add Bourbon and a lump of ice. Fill up with soda-water and serve with a twist of lemon peel.

Rye Highball
1 measure Rye whisky; Angostura; ginger ale; lemon juice.
   Mix the whisky with a dash of bitters and a squeeze of lemon juice in a tumbler. Add ice. Fill up with ginger ale.

Singapore Sling
1 measure gin; ¾ measure cherry brandy; ½ measure lemon juice; Angostura; 1 teaspoon sugar; soda-water.
   Mix the sugar, lemon and a dash of bitters in a tumbler. Add gin and cherry brandy and ice. Fill up with soda-water.

Mexican Hat
1 measure of Dubonnet; 1 small bottle bitter lemon.
   Put some ice in a tumbler, add Dubonnet and fill with bitter lemon.

Sweet Martini
2 parts gin; 1 part Italian sweet vermouth; Angostura bitters.
   Mix gin, vermouth and a dash of bitters with some cracked ice. Strain and serve.

Gin Fizz
1 measure gin; 1 teaspoon sugar; lemon juice; soda-water.
   Stir sugar, gin and lemon juice in a tumbler. Add ice and top up with soda-water.

Horse's Neck

1 measure brandy; ginger ale; Angostura.

Pour brandy into a long glass with some ice. Add a dash of Angostura. Fill up with ginger ale.

Bloody Mary

2 measures vodka; small bottle tomato juice; celery salt.

Mix vodka, tomato juice and a pinch of celery salt, together with cracked ice. Strain and serve.

Pink Gin

1 measure gin; Angostura bitters.

Shake two or three dashes of Angostura into the glass. Rotate glass. Add gin, ice and water to taste.

Wines with your meal: The subject of wines is a vast and complex one, and so much is written and talked about it that the average person can be forgiven for being somewhat confused. But it is possible to reduce the subject to certain straightforward essentials.

The first classification of wines is by colour. There are two main groups – red and white – although a few *rosé*, i.e. pink wines are available, and the sparkling wines, of which champagne is the most famous.

Next, wines are either sweet or dry. White wines range from very dry to almost cloyingly sweet. Most red wines tend to be dry, but some are sweet, particularly the dessert wines. Dry and sweet *rosés* are available.

The date when the wines were pressed is also important in the case of most (though not quite all) wines, because vintages of some years are definitely superior to those of others.

And, finally, a wine is classified according to its place of origin. Wine is produced in many countries in both the Old and the New Worlds, but it still remains true that all the world's greatest wines are produced in Western Europe, and the most famous wine-producing country of all is France.

The two greatest French wine-producing areas are

Bordeaux and Burgundy. From Bordeaux come the finest and most famous red wines in the world – they are a light, clean red, and are known as clarets. Burgundy reds are fuller, sweeter, heavier, with a stronger bouquet. White wines, both sweet and dry, are produced in both regions. They are called quite simply Bordeaux or Burgundy whites. Although nowhere near ranking in importance with these two, there is another area that deserves mention, and that is the valley of the Rhône, for the phrase Côtes du Rhône is being seen more and more on wine bottles in Britain. And, of course, there is that most famous of all sparkling wines, produced around Rheims – champagne.

But although France produces most of the great wines of the world, she does not quite produce them all. In and around the Rhineland area of Germany are made the finest of white wines – the hocks and the Moselles. These have a taste quite distinctive from any of those produced in France – much sharper and fresher. But, strangely enough, this area produces no reds of note.

The third wine-producing country of importance is Italy, whose fame has been spread by those distinctive wicker-clad bottles of Chianti, the wine from Tuscany. Chianti is, of course, but one of many reds and whites produced in Italy, but, while these are excellent of their kind they never quite reach the heights of the great French and German wines.

The fame of Spain and Portugal as wine-producers rests mainly on sherry and port, respectively, but they also produce many table wines.

Other wine-producing countries include Yugoslavia, Switzerland, Greece, and the "newer" countries of Australia, the United States (California) and South Africa.

So we come to the vexed question of what wine to drink with what food. The simplest way is to follow your own tastes and those of your guests. Drink with your food whatever wine gives you most pleasure.

CHAMPAGNE CHAMPAGNE COCKTAIL PONY TUMBLER LIQUEUR

You will probably find, however, that the reds do not go well with fish, and that a sweet wine tastes better with the fruit or dessert. But if you want the traditional rules, they are: Soup – nothing; fish – a dry white; chicken and other white meats – a dry white, particularly one of the more solid ones, or a light red; red meat – any red wine; game – a strong red; sweets and desserts – a sweet white; fruit and nuts – a sweet white, port or madeira; cheese – practically any wine.

A *rosé* is often ordered as a compromise when half the guests at a table are eating a meal calling for a white, and the others food for which a red would be more suitable, but this is not a practice approved by gourmets.

As for temperatures, a white wine or a *rosé* should be served chilled (certainly nowhere near frozen) and restaurants often place it at the table in an ice bucket. A red wine should be at room temperature. But, whatever the wine, it will be improved through having been opened in plenty of time. You should uncork your bottle as much as an hour before you expect to be pouring your first glass to your friends.

Today it is possible to buy good cheap wines from most reputable wine merchants. They will probably not have fancy names, but will most likely be varieties of *ordinaire*.

Port: This is the after-dinner drink of great English

PORT SHERRY WINE LONG DRINKS & BEER HOCK BRANDY OLD-FASHIONED

tradition, redolent of Victorian and Edwardian dinners, with the ladies retiring, and the men left behind round the table to pass the bottle and talk, until it is all brought to an end by that phrase heard in a hundred Edwardian dramas "Shall we join the ladies?" It is now enjoying something of a revival. Vintage port is made exclusively of grapes from one year, and it is the dark drink with the heavy crust. This crust must not enter the glass, which is why vintage port requires such careful storing, handling, and decanting. "Vintage type" port is blended from several years, but is treated like vintage wine; tawny port is blended from wines of different years, and ruby is a sweeter blend.

Brandy: Cognac is the most famous brandy, and it is rated from one to five stars. A three star brandy from a reputable firm would be something you could offer to your friends with confidence. The other great French brandy is Armagnac, and brandies also come from Spain, Cyprus and South Africa.

Liqueurs: The alternative to brandy is a liqueur. There are a great number of them from many parts of the world, such as Benedictine, Cointreau, Crème de Menthe, Strega, Drambuie, Advocaat, Maraschino. Which you prefer is a matter of personal taste.

121

Punches and summer cups: At parties, particularly during the winter, it is a good idea to serve punches or fruit cups. Here are some typical recipes.

Rum Punch

1 bottle rum; 1 wineglass brandy; 2–3 wineglasses water; juice of 1 orange and 1 lemon; 1 tablespoon sugar.

Place all ingredients in a heavy saucepan. Bring to the boil. Serve immediately.

Jolly Roger

1 bottle red wine; $\frac{1}{2}$ wineglass brandy; 1 tablespoon sugar; nutmeg; 1 egg.

Pour wine and brandy into a heavy saucepan. Add sugar and grated nutmeg. Heat, but don't allow to boil. Just before serving, add a well-beaten egg.

Red Velvet

1 bottle red Bordeaux wine; 1 tablespoon sugar; lemon; cinnamon.

Bring the wine, sugar and grated cinnamon to near boiling point. Strain. Serve with a slice of melon in each glass.

Blue Beat

6 parts of rum; 4 parts grenadine syrup; 2 parts lemon juice; 8 parts water; dash of dry sherry.

Stir all ingredients with ice in bowl and serve.

Hot Ale Punch

2 pints of mild ale; 1 wineglass sherry; 1 wineglass brandy; juice and peel of 1 lemon; 1 tablespoon sugar; a little grated nutmeg.

Mix all the ingredients together. Bring to the boil. Serve hot.

Mulled Claret

1 quart claret; 4 cloves; $\frac{1}{2}$ lemon sliced; cinnamon stick; 2 oz. sugar.

Gently heat all the ingredients together – do not allow to boil. Serve hot.

Champagne cup

1 bottle of champagne; 4 measures brandy; 2 measures Curaçao; dash of Maraschino; fresh fruit; soda-water – large bottle.

Stir the ingredients with ice, adding the soda-water last. Decorate with slices of orange, pineapple and a few grapes.

Claret Cup

1 bottle claret; 4 measures brandy; 2 measures Curaçao; 2 measures sherry; siphon of soda-water; fresh fruit.

Stir ingredients with cracked ice, decorate with sliced orange and lemon and a sprig of borage.

White Wine Cup

1 bottle dry white wine; 2 tablespoons brandy; 2 table-spoons Curaçao; ½ pint soda-water; fruit.

Pour the wine, brandy and Curaçao into a tall jug and chill in the refrigerator for about an hour. Before serving add the soda-water and decorate with slices of fruit and cucumber.

Home-made wines: More wines are imported into Britain today than ever before – and at cheaper prices, but anyone who drinks wine regularly should consider making his own. How much does home-made wine cost? It is impossible to be specific about this, because it depends on how much wine is made at a time and whether the basic ingredients are bought from the local shop or in bulk from farms, or grown in the garden. As an example, some home wine makers claim they do it for as little as one shilling a bottle.

The basic equipment: For making wine at home the following equipment is necessary: a bucket with a lid, or a bowl with a cloth to cover it; a large colander; a large sieve; a large funnel; a piece of rubber tubing about 6 ft. long; gallon bottles in which the wine will ferment; fermentation air locks; wine bottles; a large bottle-brush with which to clean the bottles; new corks – do not be tempted to use old ones, since they are not airtight and may carry bacteria from a previous bottle; a corking device – corks cannot be inserted satisfactorily by hand; filter bags and filter medium; foil caps for a neat finish; finally – and most important – labels, so that you will know what you are drinking.

A specialist supplier of this equipment is W. R. Loftus Ltd., 1 Charlotte St., London W.1. Chemists often sell gallon jars, and it is usually possible to persuade a sympathetic publican or restaurant owner to part with a supply of empty bottles. These, like every other item of equipment that is used for making home-made wine, should be thoroughly cleaned and sterilized. This is not merely a matter of hygiene, although that is an important aspect of the matter: it is necessary to ensure that no harmful processes are set up in the wine.

Types of home-made wine: There are now two types of home-made wine. First, there are what are known as country wines, which often make use of age-old recipes in which the fruits and crops of the English countryside, instead of the grapes of warmer countries, are used to make a liquor. Second, in recent years another method has grown up, and wines made in this way are often referred to as sophisticated home-made wines, to distinguish them from their country cousins. These make use of concentrated essences of grape juice, imported from the Continent, and the usual method is to buy a kit from a specialist supplier, which contains the juice and everything needed for making the wine. It is possible with these kits to make wines that can take the place of the red and white table wines, and even sparkling wines, vermouths, and ports.

The basic method: There are certain basic principles for home wine making, and here they are. Where, however, any variations are indicated in a specific recipe, always follow the instructions given in the recipe. First prepare the fruit. Add the water required, then the sugar and the yeast, and a yeast nutrient, which gives greater strength to the finished wine. Stir or agitate this first wash at least once a day. Ferment for up to ten days in the covered bowl, or bucket with the lid on, at about 70 degrees F. – any reasonably warm place in the house will do. The resultant liquid is called must. It should be strained through the funnel and sieved into a gallon jar, which is filled to within ¾ in. of the cork. Fit the fermentation trap to protect the wine from infection. Store the jar in a room with a temperature somewhere between 65 and 75 degrees F., and allow the fermentation to continue. It will do so for some weeks. When the fermentation has ceased, the wine should be "racked". This consists of siphoning off the wine into a clean jar with the aid of the rubber tube. Ideally the bottle should be topped up to the same level as before, which means racking wine from two bottles. Refit the fermentation trap, and repeat the whole process when the wine has cleared completely, usually about two months later. When there is no more fermentation, and no more bubbles are passing through the air lock, the wine can be bottled. Store it in a cool place – at a temperature somewhere between 55 to 65 degrees F.

Some general tips: Make sure everything is clean, and never let the wine come into contact with metal. Always use new corks and stoppers. Use best quality ingredients – this is essential for perfect results. The really top-line amateur wine makers grow all their own fruit, so that nothing is left to chance, and some even keep their own bees to make sure they have only the best honey for making mead. The term "yeast" is used throughout this section. By this is meant a proper wine yeast (which comes with full instructions) wherever possible. If a proper wine yeast cannot be obtained locally, use one level teaspoon of granulated yeast per gallon. Do not make wines too sweet. A wine that is too dry for individual tastes can always be sweetened later on. There is nothing that can be done about a wine that is over sweet to the palate: it cannot be made drier. As a general guide, it is found that 2½ lb. of sugar to the gallon makes a dry wine, 3 lb. makes a medium dry, and 3½ lb. a sweet wine. Some amateurs, impatient to be tasting their first wine, try to speed up the fermentation process by adding extra quantities of yeast. This is a mistake, as it impairs the quality of the finished wine. Keep an eye on your wine while it is fermenting. It should never stand for long on a sediment of dead yeast. Rack it twice or three times if this is necessary. Finally, do not be impatient to open a bottle and serve the wine. Leave it for at least six months and longer if possible. Most country white wines are at their best after maturing for six months, red wines after two years. Here are some specimen recipes.

ELDERBERRY

4 lb. elderberries; 3½ lb. white sugar; 1 gallon water; yeast and nutrient.

Strip the berries from the stalk with an ordinary fork. Weigh them and crush them. Pour on the boiling water and let it cool to about 70 degrees F. before adding the yeast. Leave for three days, stirring daily, then strain on to the sugar. Pour the liquor into a one-gallon bottle and fit the fermentation trap, but do not fill it completely until the first vigorous fermentation has subsided. When the fermentation has settled down a bit, the gallon bottle can be filled properly, and the trap re-fitted. Use dark bottles for this wine, for it may lose its colour in clear ones.

BLACKBERRY

4 lb. blackberries; 3 lb. granulated sugar; 1 gallon water; yeast and nutrient.

Use fresh blackberries if you can, picking them when they are ripe. The fruit needs to be well washed. Keep a lookout for those small maggots that are often found on blackberries. Crush the blackberries with a wooden spoon and pour a gallon of boiling water over them, then stir well. When the temperature has fallen to 70 degrees F., add the yeast. Leave the mixture to ferment, keeping it well covered, and stir it each day. Then strain it on to the sugar and add the yeast nutrient, stirring well to make sure that it is all dissolved. Then fill the fermenting jar to the

126

shoulder, and fit the trap. Keep the liquor that is left over in a smaller bottle. It will be necessary also to fit a fermentation air lock to this. After about a week, the fermentation will have settled down enough and there will be no risk of the liquor bubbling up through the air traps. The spare liquor can then be added to the gallon jar.

CHERRY

6 lb. black cherries; 4 lb. preserving sugar; 1 gallon water; yeast and nutrient.

Crush the cherries, taking care not to break any of the stones, and leave them to soak for 48 hours in boiling water. Strain it well. Bring the juice to boiling point and pour it over the sugar, stirring well until all the sugar is dissolved. Add the yeast once the liquid has cooled. Cover it and allow it to ferment in a warm place for 14 days, then put it into a fermenting bottle with trap.

MEAD

$3\frac{1}{2}$–4 lb. mild honey; $\frac{1}{2}$ oz. citric acid; 1 gallon water; yeast and nutrient.

Use $3\frac{1}{2}$ or 4 lb. of honey, according to how sweet or dry you want the mead to be. If a wine yeast is being used, have it activated and ready in advance. Bring the honey to the boil in two or three times its own volume of water, stirring with a wooden spoon until all the honey is dissolved – otherwise it may burn – and skimming off any scum that rises to the top of the water. The yeast nutrient is added to the hot liquid, and the rest of the water can be added when convenient. When the liquid is cool, add the yeast, and place it in the fermentation vessel, fitting the air lock. A gallon of water and a few pounds of honey will add up to 9 or 10 pints of liquid, but this will come down to a gallon once racking has been carried out. This should be done when the wine is beginning to clear, and you can see a definite sludge forming at the bottom of the bottle. Old country recipes recommend keeping mead for years – as long as seven, even, but one year is long enough.

ORANGE

12 sweet oranges; $3\frac{1}{2}$ lb. white sugar; 1 gallon water; yeast and nutrient.

Peel thinly six of the oranges, and pour a quart of boiling

water on to the rind. It is important that only the rind be cut from the oranges. The pith adds a bitter taste to the wine. After the liquid has stood for 24 hours, strain off the water into a bowl which contains the remaining three quarts of water and the sugar. Cut all the oranges in half, and squeeze the juice into yeast. If a general wine yeast has been used, the liquor can safely be strained off into a bottle, and a trap fitted, within two or three days. Siphon for the first time when it clears.

RHUBARB

6 lb. red rhubarb; 3½ lb. white sugar; 2 or 3 lemons; 1 gallon water; yeast and nutrient.

Clean the rhubarb by wiping it with a damp cloth. Cut it into short lengths, and crush it with a clean piece of hardboard. Pour the water over it cold, and add a crushed Campden tablet to the liquid. The liquid should now be left covered for three days, and it should be stirred several times a day. Then strain and squeeze the pulp as dry as possible. There is far too much acid in rhubarb, and this has a distinctly unpleasant taste. It can be removed, however, if at this stage you add 1 oz. of precipitated chalk, which can be had from the chemist. Do not worry as the juice fizzes when you add the chalk – this is quite normal. Once the fizzing has stopped, you can taste to see if there is still a trace of acid. If there is, a further ½ oz. of the precipitated chalk can be added. Now add the sugar, the yeast, the nutrient, and the juice of the lemons. Pour into a fermenting vessel, and fit an air lock, but keep half a pint or so of the liquid separate. This should be kept in a bottle, preferably with its own trap, but, at a pinch it could be plugged with cotton wool instead. This liquid is used to top up the large jar when the fermentation quietens off. Leave until the wine begins to clear, and then rack for the first time. At this stage, if you wish, you can add half a dozen clean broken egg shells to remove all colour from the wine.

PARSNIP, sometimes called Tanglefoot.

7 lb. parsnips; 3 lb. sugar for each gallon of liquid; 2½ gallons of water; 2 lemons; yeast and nutrient.

The parsnips must be scrubbed, scraped, sliced and boiled in the water. The boiling should stop when the parsnips are tender, but before they are mushy. Strain the liquor, and add the sugar and the juice of the lemons. Bring it once again to the boil, and let it simmer for three-quarters of an hour. It can then be poured into a crock, and allowed to cool down to 70 degrees F., when the yeast and yeast nutrient should be added. Then keep covered in a warm place for a week, stirring well from the bottom each day. It can then be strained into a fermenting jar.

CYSER (Note: this is correct spelling. It isn't Cyder)

1 lb. crab or cooking apples; 3 lb. honey; 1 gallon water; yeast and nutrient.

The apples must be washed and crushed with a piece of heavy timber, and then the juice squeezed out. There are two ways of doing this. A press (buy them at any supplier of wine-making equipment) can be used; or the apples can be wrapped in a cloth and kneaded over a bowl. The resultant juice is then added to the honey, and the whole lot boiled in the water. Allow it to simmer for two or three minutes, then skim off any scum. The yeast and nutrient can be added once the liquid has cooled off to 70 degrees F. Now pour it into a bottle, with trap, to ferment. It should be left to mature, once it has been finally bottled, for a year.

GRAPE

6 lb. grapes (any sort); 1 gallon water; 3 lb. white sugar; yeast and nutrient.

This is your chance to try your hand at making "real" wine. Crush each grape with your finger and thumb, and cover them all with cold water. Add a Campden tablet, and cover the liquid. A day later, add the yeast. Stir and mash the grapes each day for seven days, then strain them on to the sugar, and stir well, until all the sugar has been dissolved. Pour into the fermenting jar, and treat in the usual way.

ELDERFLOWER

$\frac{2}{3}$ pint of elderflower; 1 gallon water; 3 lb. (for dry) or $3\frac{3}{4}$ lb. (for sweet) white sugar; $\frac{1}{2}$ lb. chopped raisins; juice of three lemons, yeast and nutrient.

It is important not to add less than 3 lb. of sugar, other-wise the wine will be too dry to be palatable, and not to use more than the specified amount of elderflower, or the wine will acquire an unpleasantly pungent bouquet. The flowers should be gathered on a sunny day when they are fully opened, trimmed from the stem with scissors, and placed in a jar until there is the required amount of florets, not pressed down. The sugar, chopped raisins and lemon juice can then be added to the flowers, and boiling water poured over the lot. Cool the liquid to 70 degrees F., add the yeast nutrient, and a level teaspoon of granulated yeast. Leave it to ferment, covered, for four to five days, in a warm place. Strain it, leave it to ferment, and rack and bottle normally.

In the Garden

Making a new lawn: Turfing is a quick way of getting a ready-to-use lawn of tough, hard-wearing properties but of inferior quality. The lawn site must first be adjusted for levels which should be struck from the house end by setting out pegs at six-foot intervals, and checking them with straight-edge and spirit level. The soil should be very thoroughly worked over, removing roots, stones and large clumps of earth, until a fine tilth is achieved. Heel-tread the ground, finding the soft spots and raking in soil to make them good. Heel-treading is far more effective than rolling initially, which serves its purpose just before the final raking. If the soil is exceptionally heavy, a 2-in. layer of topsoil will have to be spread over the lawn site. This will give the right conditions for rapid root development. The ideal lawn bed only leaves the slightest imprint when walked upon. Prior to turfing, a pre-seeding base fertilizer should be raked into the top half an inch of soil.

Laying the turves: Lay boards on the first row of turves and move down on to subsequent rows as the work proceeds. In this way, partial consolidation is carried out at the same time. Turves should be bonded like bricks so that no joints coincide. When three-quarters of the lawn has been completed, start laying from the other end, so that any irregular spaces are made up well within the general lawn area and not on the edges.

Thoroughly consolidate the turves with a wooden thumper and finish off with a final roll. The lawn should not be cut until the turves are well rooted, which takes some four to six weeks, according to weather conditions. No selective weedkillers should be applied to the turf for at least six months. It is a wise precaution to ensure that the new turves have been treated prior to lifting, since most meadow-grown turf is very weedy.

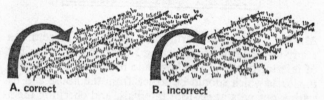

A. correct   B. incorrect

There is a right and a wrong method of laying turves

Seeding a lawn: Seeding is undoubtedly the best way to achieve a good quality lawn if one is prepared for the amount of after-attention that is required. To ensure the uninterrupted development of the new grasses, a newly seeded lawn cannot be used for at least six months after seeding.

The proposed lawn site should be thoroughly cultivated. If the ground is very heavy, incorporate plenty of gritty material, such as fine coke breeze, coarse sand, well-rotted manure, or compost. Granulated peat, raked into the top surface with a pre-seeding fertilizer, will ensure rapid rooting and good moisture retention. Weeds are the major problem when seeding a lawn on a new site. Fallowing is the most effective way of dealing with them, if time and patience permit. Rough-level the seed-bed in the spring, and by alternate hoeings and rakings from May until August the weeds will be destroyed.

Prepare the seed-bed in September by alternate cross-raking and rolling, reducing the soil to a very fine tilth. Good quality lawn-seed, with a harmless bird repellent added to it, should be got from a reliable garden sundries-man, together with a pre-seeding fertilizer.

Broadcasting of the seed can be carried out by hand or by using a fertilizer distributor set to spread at the rate of 2 oz. per square yard. Uniform manual sowing is vital to combat weeds and to get a satisfactory sward. Divide the seed into two equal amounts and sow first in one direction and then the other. A more laborious, but effective method, is to divide the area to be sown into a number of spaces, and divide the seed into double this number of (equal) small lots. Then sow each space in cross directions. The seed should be sown on a raked surface and raked very lightly into the soil, which should then be rolled – provided that dry conditions prevail.

Given good weather, germination should take place in ten to twelve days, and the first cut can be made when the grass is about 2 in. high. It is best to use a mower with a rotary blade, as this will not tear at the sward. A spring fertilizer is beneficial after an autumn sowing and should be applied in March or April when more frequent mowings can take place.

With a spring-sown lawn, it must be remembered that rapid weed-growth will accompany seed germination; where infestation is particularly bad, the larger weeds should be carefully removed, using boards over the new grass. No selective weed-killers should be applied to seeded lawns for at least 12 months from the time of sowing.

Care of the Lawn: There is immense satisfaction in creating a luxuriant, rich green lawn. This can be achieved by anybody who is prepared to observe a few simple principles from the outset. In the early spring the lawn should be spiked and there are a number of excellent implements on the market which make light work of this rather tedious operation. After spiking the lawn apply a dressing of lawn sand. The quickest and easiest way to do this is to use one of the fertilizer spreaders. One of the

Proper spiking is an important part of lawn maintenance

most important operations, particularly in the spring and early summer, is the brushing up of the grass. This makes the coarse grasses stand up to meet the mower blades, and it also revitalizes the turf after the winter. Light work can be made of brushing by using one of the rotary lawn sweepers. Brushing up the grass should be carried out at least every other cut, and spiking should continue through the summer at least once a month. If infested with weeds, use a selective weed-killer. After applying selective weed-killer according to the makers' instructions, the lawn should receive an application of fertilizer about three weeks later.

In dry weather the lawn must be watered regularly to maintain both its root growth and colour. There is an excellent selection of sprinklers on the market of both the rotary and square area types.

Preparing flower borders: Heavy clay is the legacy of much house-building and one must be realistic from the very beginning in dealing with it. Firstly, it must be lightened with gritty material, peat and compost. If the ground is excessively heavy, there is a more economical way of preparing places for plants and shrubs. Dig out each planting-hole separately, thoroughly breaking up the bottom of it. Then fill the hole with equal parts peat, or leaf-mould, and good topsoil, adding a generous supply of manure or compost to the bottom of the hole. Set the plants firmly in these holes and at least they will have the opportunity of thriving in reasonable soil conditions.

The ideal method, if enthusiasm will permit, is to trench the ground at least one spit deep and add plenty of gritty material such as coke breeze, coarse sand, rubble and well-rotted manure or compost. Granulated peat in the top surface is ideal for rooting. Dig each trench across the plot, throwing the earth forward from the next trench and thoroughly mixing it with your lightening material.

The earth excavated from the first trench should be used to fill in the final trench at the far end of the plot. One word of warning: never use fresh coke breeze, as it retains gases which are harmful to plants. Be on the look-out for dry spells, especially in the early spring and summer. Let the hose lie at the base of each plant for a time and make a shallow bowl round the base of the stem

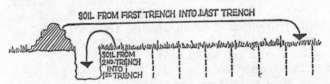

SOIL FROM FIRST TRENCH INTO LAST TRENCH

SOIL FROM 2ND-TRENCH INTO 1ST TRENCH

to trap the water. A sprinkler is most useful during the summer months, and you should let it play on the lawn and borders all day (altering the position every two hours) when the weather is exceptionally dry.

Light, sandy soils require plenty of humus in order to retain moisture and body. Well-rotted garden compost or, preferably, manure worked into the ground each autumn,

135

will gradually give a steady moisture and nourishment content to what would otherwise be unproductive ground.

Spring-flowering borders: There are two ways of arranging spring-flowering bulbs to give eye-catching colour displays: 1. By close planting of individual varieties, 4 to 5 in. apart; 2. By increasing the distance between the bulbs to 6 or 8 in. and planting out with ground-cover subjects which will add to the overall colour theme and keep early-season weed-growth under control.

Here are some planting schemes which, with good ground-cover interplanting, you can employ in your own garden, and they will give that little touch of originality and life:

Tulip Wintergold interplanted with Muscari armeniacum (grape hyacinth); Tulip Ibis interplanted with grape hyacinth; Tulip Kaufmanniana interplanted with Primula denticulata; Narcissus (Poetas) geranium interplanted with wallflower Scarlet Bedder; Tulip (Darwin) Pride of Zwannenberg interplanted with Arabis albida; Tulip (Cottage) Northern Queen interplanted with deep blue pansies; Tulip (Triumph) Orange Korneforos interplanted with Arabis albida; Tulip (Triumph) Bruno Walter interplanted with pansies (variety Ullswater); Daffodils (Golden Harvest or Rembrandt) interplanted with polyanthus in mixed colours. Hyacinth Pink Pearl interplanted with forget-me-nots. Daffodils or narcissi interplanted with wallflowers.

In window boxes, hanging baskets and free-standing plant containers, the following schemes could be used:

Pheasant's eye narcissi interplanted with mixed polyanthus; Daffodil Golden Harvest interplanted with Primula wanda; Tulip (Prince of Orange) interplanted with Scilla siberica; Crocuses, grape hyacinths, chionodoxa interplanted with Primula wanda and primroses; Mixed narcissi interplanted with wallflowers.

Summer borders: Summer bedding plants offer a wide variety of colour patterns and combinations. At the end of the bulb season, carefully lift the bulbs and store them in boxes filled with peat.

Antirrhinums (variety Bonfire) form a pleasing colour scheme when their deep red is offset by an interplanting of tagetes. Petunias (variety Capri), interplanted with salvias (variety Blaze of Fire), make an impressive show. An edging to this layout could be either ageratum or purple lobelia.

Fuchsias add both height and dignity to the summer border and cuttings can be taken from each plant later in the season. Take the cuttings and put them in the soil where the plants are growing. By the end of the summer you will have many rooted cuttings (they may even have flowered) which only need to be potted and put in a greenhouse for the winter.

The dwarf sweet pea (variety Bijou) should not be forgotten. It does remarkably well in places where you want plenty of ground cover and strong colour since it spreads widely. Plant it on banks and in odd corners where it can grow freely.

Good, strong, background colours can be provided by the magnificent selection of Coltness hybrid dahlias. These will go on flowering continually and profusely until the first frosts. Lift the tubers, then store them in boxes for the winter. The giant cactus flowering dahlias give excellent and impressive background colour where height is needed to hide walls. Give them good staking.

As a border edging, ageratum with a backing of dwarf early-flowering chrysanthemums, and a further background of zinnias, will give you a splendid display throughout the season. Geraniums, interplanted with French marigolds and the beautiful coloured-leaf plant coleus, form a striking and unusual border combination. Salvias, interplanted with French marigolds, are also effective, but do not plant them under or near trees.

Where you have deep borders, an inexpensive way of

covering them with carpets of colour is to set out mass blocks of lobelia, ageratum, alyssum, French marigolds, tagetes and bedding begonias. Soon you will have great carpets of bright bloom which will also restrict weeds.

The large-flowering begonias are effective in a summer border when interplanted with fuchsias. These will stand above the begonias and show their blooms to advantage while the begonias' blooms will give colour closer to the ground. Large-flowering begonias are not suitable for exposed sites, as high winds tend to break the soft stems and the blooms fall off very easily. Pinch out secondary blooms as they appear on each side of the main flower. This gives the best results for flowering.

Summer-flowering chrysanthemums, particularly the mid-season varieties, give an excellent colour arrangement. They can form the background to geraniums or salvias which can be fronted by ageratum or a mixed selection of nemesias.

Flower beds containing one variety, or species, can be very effective. For example, antirrhinums in single blocks of colour can be set out in beds along a garage frontage with a centrepiece of hydrangea or a half-standard fuchsia in each bed. This applies also to geraniums, salvias, begonias or any of the strong colour plants which will liven up a dead space.

Roses are among the most rewarding plants for summer colour and require little maintenance.

Young bedding plants are an easy prey for slugs, so use a slug-destroyer immediately after planting.

The Shrub border: Here is a selection of flowering and evergreen shrubs which will give colour and scent to your borders throughout the season.

Scented Shrubs: Azalea (deciduous); Berberis stenophylla; Buddleia; Choisya; Daphne; Eucryphia; Genista aetnensis; Hamamelis; Jasmine; Lavender; Lonicera (Honeysuckle); Mahonia Bealei; Magnolia; Osmarea burkwoodii; Philadelphus; Rhododendron loderi; Rose-mary; Rosa hybrid musk; Santolina; Syringa (Lilac); Viburnum caricephalum; Viburnum fragrans; Wisteria.

Shrubs for town and industrial areas: Acer (except Negundo and Palmatum varieties); Azalea; Aesculus; Ash; Ampelopsis; Betula alba varieties; Berberis aquifolium; Berberis stenophylla; Berberis darwinii; Buxus (Box); Chaenomeles (all varieties); Contoneaster (all varieties); Cornus; Crataegus oxycantha; Deutzia; Diervilla; Euonymus; Forsythia; Gingko biloba; Hypericum; Kerria japonica; Laburnum; Malus (in variety); Olearia haastii; Pernettya; Philadelphus; Pyracantha; Prunus; Rhus typhina; Roses (all types); Sorbus; Syringa (all varieties); Veronica traversii; Viburnum (all varieties); Yucca.

Shrubs for shaded positions: (Those marked (t) may be grown under trees). Acer (Japanese varieties) (t); Azalea; Berberis mahonia (t); Buxus (Box) (t); Camellia; Chaenomeles; Choisya; Cornus alba (varieties); Cotoneaster (t); Daphne (t); Enkianthus; Gaultheria; Hedera (Ivy) (t); Hydrangea Blue Wave; Hypericum (t); Ilex (Holly) (not golden varieties) (t); Kerria; Laurel; Ligustrum (t); Lonicera; Olearia haastii; Osmarea; Pernettya (t); Pyracantha; Rhododendron (t); Ribes (t); Sambucus (t); Spiraea Anthony Waterer; Viburnum (winter-flowering varieties) (t); Vinca (t).

Shrubs for chalky soils: Acer (in variety); Aesculus; Ash (fraxinus); Beech; Berberis; Betula; Buddleia; Chaenomeles; Choisya; Cistus; Clematis; Cornus; Cotoneaster; Crataegus; Daphne; Deutzia; Diervilla; Escallonia; Euonymus europaeus; Erica (of sorts); Forsythia; Fuchsia; Hornbeam (Carpinus); Hypericum; Ilex (Holly); Laburnum; Laurel; Malus; Philadelphus; Paeony (Tree); Potentilla; Prunus (all sections); Rhus; Ribes; Senecio; Sorbus; Spiraea; Syringa (Lilac); Veronica; Viburnum.

For the Rose Garden: Pink – Ballet, Grace de Monaco, My Choice, Silver Lining, Stella. Carmine – Eden Rose, Rose Gaujard, Wendy Cussons. Red – Christian Dior,

Ena Harkness, Uncle Walter, Westminster. Yellow to Orange – Beaute, Gold Crown, Lady Belper, Peace, Piccadilly, Spek's Yellow. Flame and vermilion – Mischief, Mrs. Sam McGredy, Super Star. White – Frau Karl Druschki.

A dressing of bonemeal will give the roses a good start and two or three further applications during the season will keep up the colour impact.

Fruit trees: Great care must be taken when choosing fruit trees that you buy varieties which are either self-fertile or will cross-pollinate with a different variety of the same fruit in blossom at the same time. Cox's Orange Pippin apple, for example, is not self-fertile, and for this reason it should never be grown in the garden as a single specimen. Self-fertile apples which can be grown as single specimens are Reverend W. Wilks, Laxton's Superb, Laxton's Epicure and Lord Derby. Always plant for a good succession of fruit so that the harvesting does not result in a glut of fruit with which it is impossible to cope. Laxton's Epicure is an early apple which could be followed by Egremont Russet and later still Laxton's Superb. Cox's Orange Pippin, James Grieve and Laxton's Epicure are particularly good for home consumption.

Black currants: Plant two-year-old bushes 5 ft. apart each way in well cultivated soil. Pruning is carried out immediately after the bushes have fruited, and consists of cutting out completely the old fruiting wood and leaving only the strongest of the new shoots to develop for next season's fruit bearing. Cut out all overcrowding branches at this time and again in the winter if they develop after the first pruning. Seabrook's Black and Boskoop Giant are among the best for home use.

Red and white currants: Buy two-year-old bushes and plant them 5 ft. apart. Prune back the main stems and remove all weak, straggly growth. It is sufficient to leave three or four buds on each lateral growth. Bear in mind that red currants fruit on the old wood and not on the new as do black currants. Good varieties to choose are White Dutch, Red Dutch and Raby Castle.

Gooseberries: Plant two- or three-year-old bushes 5 ft. apart. Gooseberries can tolerate a good deal of shade, so they are useful space-fillers under trees. Prune the bushes in March, merely thinning out branches to admit sunlight and air. Gooseberries fruit prolifically, and they do not require quite such detailed pruning as do other fruit bushes.

Raspberries: Raspberries are one of the most rewarding of fruits in the home garden. They are always expensive in the shops, and have lost their best flavour by the time they reach the retailer. Buy good quality, disease-free raspberry canes and plant them in rows 4 ft. apart and 18 in. between the canes. Support the canes on wires, stretched between 4-ft. high posts running the length of the rows. At the end of the season cut the old canes which have fruited down to ground level and leave the new shoots to develop for next year's fruit-bearing. Tie in the new canes as they mature to keep the rows tidy and to facilitate harvesting of the crop the next summer. Good varieties are Malling Exploit and Lloyd George.

Strawberries: Strawberries are well worth growing provided that you have the time and patience to give them the attention which they require. You can purchase plants in September or March and plant them 18 in apart in rows 2 ft. apart. During the growing season the new plants will send out runners on which new plants develop. Pot up these new plants in a rich soil and plant out when strong roots have developed.

Strawberry plants have a fruitful life cycle of three years, after which they should be scrapped. It is a good plan to do away with one-third of the strawberry bed each year and replace it with the plants obtained from the runners earlier in the season. Never strike plants on runners growing from an unfruitful parent plant, as it will only repeat the sterile process. Straw must be laid down between the rows before the fruits develop to any size, and great care must be taken not to damage them in the process. Soft fruit in the small garden is always a worthwhile crop. It is expensive in the shops, owing to the high cost of harvesting, and the flavour of home-grown soft fruit is different from anything which your green-grocer can produce.

Spraying fruit trees and bushes: In order to spray fruit trees effectively you must have spraying equipment powerful enough to drench the entire tree. Give all fruit trees and bushes a thorough soaking of tar oil winter wash in December. Avoid carrying out spraying on windy or frosty days or if heavy rain is forecast. Tar oil is messy to use if it is blown all over the place, and will discolour grass for a month or more. A captan wash should be given to apple trees just before blossom time to counteract scab disease, and a further spraying should be given when the blossom is fully out.

Pruning fruit trees and bushes: Pruning fruit trees is not an art known only to a chosen few in the gardening world. Once you know the basic principles and techniques you will be master of the fruit garden. A knowledge of the terms applied to the different parts of a tree is essential if you are to make sense of the jargon on pruning which fills most garden books. Too often a misunderstanding of terminology has resulted in the cutting out of fruit-bearing branches and the consequent reduction in crops for several seasons. Pruning is a positive, purposeful operation with one end in view – to produce more fruit of good quality as the tree matures. To this end, pruning should be an annual affair with the exception of the first year after the planting of a new tree. One important task during the summer after planting is to remove all young fruitlets as soon as they become visible. The new tree requires all its energies for building up a healthy root and branch system in the early stages. In any event, the young branches would probably snap under the weight of fruit borne too soon.

Pruning apple trees: The three- to four-year-old trees are the best buy from the nursery, as the tricky stages of early pruning are over and the grower should have produced a good shapely tree to grace your fruit garden. After planting, refrain from pruning until the following winter, unless there are any cross-branches rubbing against each other which would cause bark wounds. Careful shaping of the young tree is of paramount importance, since this will decide the ultimate form of the subject.

As a general guide, shoots of the previous year's growth should be shortened by half to just above a bud which is pointing in the direction in which you want the branch to grow to maintain the shape of the tree. Cut close to the bud with a well-sharpened pair of secateurs, sloping in the same direction as the bud. Avoid leaving snags above the bud which will only die back and become potential harbourers of disease. Keep the centre of the tree clear of inward growing criss-cross branches, by cutting right back to their junctions with main leader branches. Seal all major cuts with white lead paint. Keep a mental picture of the ultimate shape of the tree you are pruning, and only remove those branches and shoots which will spoil the end product. Cut out suckers which grow up from the base of the stem, and burn all diseased wood. A useful tip is to pare round the edges of a major cut with a sharp pruning knife. This causes the bark to callous over quickly, healing the wound and hiding an ugly cut.

Subsequent pruning after the second year of establishment is only a matter of cutting out rubbing branches, ingrowing branches, suckers and dead snags. The centre must be thinned every three to four years to admit sunlight and air to foliage and blossom and fruit. The stake can be removed at the end of the second season, by which time the roots will have taken a firm hold. Fruit is borne on wood of a different age according to the type and variety of tree. For example, apple trees bear fruit on wood which is two years old and continue to bear on the same wood for years.

Care must be taken not to cut beyond the previous year's growth or you will impair the tree's fruiting capacity for the following season. The exception to this rule is when you are removing whole branches for thinning purposes. The same general pruning principles apply to bush, half-standard and full standard trees.

You must preserve a balance between branch thinning to admit light and air, and branch development to carry more fruiting spurs. The fruiting spur is quite easily distinguished from the leaf-bearing shoot. The former is fuller and fatter, whereas the leaf bud is small and pointed. Apple trees need open centres and long untangled leaders, bearing laterals full of fruit buds. Espalier and fan-trained trees carry their fruit on short spurs which must be encouraged to multiply by pruning back to within two buds of the previous year's growth.

Pruning pear trees: Pear trees have a more upright growth structure than apple trees and fruit spurs sprout from long continuous laterals. For this reason confine your selection to either bush, fan-trained or cordon types. Follow the general pruning principles as described above, always bearing in mind that you have to get at the fruit at harvest time and the best fruit is often at the ends of the laterals where they enjoy maximum sunlight. Keep the laterals within bounds and avoid letting them reach for the stars.

Pruning plum trees: Provided that you buy three- or

four-year-old stock from the nurseryman, plum trees require very little pruning. The plum family is particularly prone to the fatal Silver Leaf disease and hard pruning, particularly during the wintertime, is one of the surest ways of encouraging it. A certain amount of thinning may be necessary from time to time to keep the centre of the tree open, and this should be done during the summer, when the natural process of gumming will quickly seal the cuts against the spores of Silver Leaf.

Pruning cherry trees: Cherry trees bear their fruit on long delicate branches. The new wood must be retained and encouraged to develop towards the sunlight, and the old wood should be cut by at least a quarter of its length to make way for next year's fruit-bearing branches. The fruit buds are distinguishable from the leaf buds because they develop as double buds. Remember to seal up all major cuts with white lead paint. Like the plum, the cherry family is susceptible to Silver Leaf, so pruning must be minimal.

Pruning peach trees: The old wood should be cut out in April each year, and the new shoots left to develop foliage and fruit spurs. Thinning of new wood can be carried out in June if there are too many unevenly spaced branches. Seal all major cuts with white lead paint.

Pruning shrubs: In general, the small-garden shrubs require only a limited amount of attention as far as pruning is concerned. The main considerations in shrub pruning are:
1. Maintenance of the form and line characteristic of the shrub.
2. Development of the formation of flowers or berries.
3. Sustaining the vigour and vitality of the shrub.
4. Control of the size of the subject.

In the main, shrubs renew their growth by sending up stems from or near the base. The art in pruning is to know when to remove the older branches completely to make room for the new growth. Total removal of old wood should take place every three to four years, when the new stems will have become sufficiently vigorous to maintain the flower and foliage balance of the shrub. It may also be necessary to remove some of the new stems, if they are overcrowding each other or growing in towards the centre of the shrub.

The pruning technique is exactly the same as that applied to tree pruning. You should be aware of what is taking place in the system of the shrub when pruning is carried out. A certain amount of growth substance is removed with the loss of a branch or section of a branch, and, as a result, the roots die back slightly. But there is also a natural re-adjustment which takes place, inasmuch as the growth energy, previously directed towards the branch now removed, can now be concentrated upon the development of new buds, shoots, leaves and flowers.

If a shrub is becoming unbalanced in its shape, do not cut back on the side which is making the stronger growth. The reverse procedure should be adopted.

Shrubs fall into two distinct classes as far as pruning is concerned: deciduous and evergreen.

Deciduous Shrubs: These again fall into two groups:

1. Shrubs which flower on wood matured in the previous year, and which flower in the winter or spring. These shrubs require pruning only every two to three years. The work should be done immediately after flowering, thus giving the plants ample time to develop new shoots and leaves for the next year's ripening. If shrubs have been left unpruned for several years, concentrate on removing all of the oldest wood. Do not be discouraged by the sorry sight which will result from this massacre – next year's development will repay you. Certain shrubs respond well to annual pruning, particularly the Cytisus and Genista groups. With these subjects, cut the flowered shoots to their base, but leave the older wood.

Shrubs such as the Cornuses and Salix, which are grown for their coloured stems, must be cut back hard to within a bud or so of their crowns. Winter Jasmine (Jasminum nudiflorum) responds well to pruning. Cut off the flowered shoots of winter-flowering heaths (Erica carnea, etc.) in order to maintain their bushy habit. Spring-flowering Viburnums, Caragana, Deutzia, Magnolia and Syringa only require their spent flower-heads removing.

2. The second group of deciduous shrubs consists of plants which flower on wood of the current year's growth and bloom in the summer and autumn. The pruning procedure is to cut back last year's flowered shoots to within an inch or two of the previous year's wood. The following subjects come under this heading – Buddleia davidii, Caryopteris clandonensis, Ceanothus Gloire de Versaille, Hibiscus, Hydrangea paniculata, Hypericum, Indigofera, Potentilla, Sparticum junceum, Spiraea japonica, Spiraea arborea, Spiraea menziesii, Spiraea salicifolia, and Tamarix pentandra.

Evergreen shrubs: The majority of evergreen shrubs require very little attention in the way of pruning. There are one or two exceptions, such as Calluna vulgaris, which should have last year's growth cut back in April. Ceanothus Autumnal Blue and Ceanothus burkwoodii should also have last year's growth cut back hard in April. Daebaecia cantabrica, Ericas, Rosmarinus officinalis and Santolina chamaecyparissus, all respond well to trimming in the spring. It is important to remove the spent flower heads of rhododendrons and azaleas immediately so that next year's flower buds may have plenty of time to develop.

Laurels are often given up for lost when they have been allowed to go wild for many years. Severe pruning of the old wood in early spring will produce strong new growth from the base and a new hedge will very soon develop if the old growth has not been left untended for too long.

Window-boxes: The best timber to use for making a window-box is Western red cedar. It can be painted or stained to match the rest of the exterior woodwork. If ordinary softwood is used, the inside of the box should be treated with a preservative, to stop it from rotting. But ask your supplier to sell you one that is guaranteed not to be harmful to plant life.

Small boxes up to about 2ft. 6 in. long can be made of ¾-in. timber, but for lengths above this 1-in. thick timber should be bought. If a window-box is to last any length of time it needs to be soundly constructed, and the crafts-man would join the sides to the front and back by means of dovetail joints. These, however, are beyond the capabilities of most amateurs, who will want merely to nail the four pieces of wood together. In this case, it is essential that the corners should be strengthened in some way. Probably the best way of doing this is to use angle brackets – two in each corner – and these should be screwed in place inside the box. Both the brackets and screws should be galvanized to make them rust-resistant, otherwise they would soon deteriorate.

The bottom of the box, which again needs to be of ¾ in. or 1 in. material, according to the size of the box, can be merely nailed in place. A better way, however, would be to fix lengths of 1 in. sq. material along the bottom inside edges of the box, and rest the base on these. Whichever method is chosen, however, it is essential that drainage holes should be drilled in the base.

The box should be about 2 in. less than the window opening in length so that it can be easily lifted in and out of place, and it is better if its width is marginally less than that of the ledge. In older houses, the window ledge may have worn considerably, and may slope forward quite a bit. In that case, small pieces of timber should be placed underneath the box at the front edge to make sure that it is level. Wedge-shaped pieces would be best. If the box is to be above ground level, it represents a considerable hazard should it ever fall down. Some means of making sure that this does not happen is essential. An easy way is to fit an eye hook to each end of the box, and to the timber of the window-frame. A length of metal chain (which is much better than string or rope, because this might soon rot) can then be run between the two.

Before putting any soil in the box, cover with broken crocks or small pebbles the drainage holes that have been bored in the base to ensure good drainage. These should in turn be covered with peat or leaf-mould to ensure that the soil does not clog up the drainage system. The soil can now be placed in the box. This can be any good garden soil, and it is a good idea to enrich it with a little bonemeal. If, however, there is no garden from which to obtain the soil – and, in fact, the window-boxes are to be cultivated for precisely that reason – then a John Innes potting compost can be used.

There is little to do in the way of cultivation, except to see that the plants are well watered, because window-boxes dry out very quickly. As for feeding, you might as well do this at the same time as you water your plants, by using a liquid fertilizer. In any case, this is much easier to handle in the confined spaces of a window-box. It will also increase your chances of getting better blooms if you pinch off old flowers as soon as they are dead.

Compost heap: A compost heap can easily be made from garden and household waste: grass cuttings, prunings, potato peelings and outside leaves of lettuce and cabbage are ideal. Sprinkle liberally with an activator such as that made by Adco Ltd., and in 8 to 10 weeks you will have some of the most valuable manure available.

Terraces: The terraces should be built as an essential part of the garden from the outset. The terrace is fast becoming an extension of the lounge, and the transition from the one living space to the other can be exciting and effective if the design is carefully and tastefully composed.

Partial covering in the form of glass roofing and

attractive screening can make the terrace a comfortable and draught-free place, both early and late in the season.

Paved surfaces for terraces are exciting in their range and variety, thanks to the resources of the precast paving industry. Rectangular coloured paving slabs, laid in various themes and patterns, random crazy paving, either in natural or precast stone, and formal chequer-board designs with cobblestone panels, all provide a wide field of choice for the terrace-builder.

Constructing a terrace: Mark out the shape of the terrace with wooden pegs, making sure that even curves are achieved throughout, if you are adopting an informal design. Excavate the terrace site to a depth of 8 in. then lay down a 4 in. bed of coarse clinker or hardcore and consolidate it. Prepare a mortar mix consisting of 4 parts of builders' soft sand and 1 part of cement, making sure that the mix is of a good firm consistency. Bed down the stones on 2 in. of this mix.

Stones on the outer edges of the terraces should be laid first, following carefully the curves marked out by the pegs. Use larger stones on the outside edges, as this makes for greater strength at the weakest points. Levels should be checked across the area by means of pegs and spirit level so that the outer edges are true throughout. Now the inside area can be laid, and it is advisable to lay some marker stones in the central area and check their level with the outside edges.

It is a comparatively simple matter to lay the remainder of the stones, using a levelling board to check their true-ness with the outer edges and the centre stones. Leave a $\frac{1}{2}$-inch gap between the segments of paving for pointing-up. Prepare a mix consisting of 2 parts sharp sand and 1 part cement, and fill the gaps between the stones, bringing the mix flush with the top of the paving and shaping along the edge of each stone with the pointing-trowel so that there is a clean joint and good adherence.

Ensure that there is an even distribution of stone sizes –

not unsightly groupings of very small pieces or the reverse. Where the paving is laid against the face of the house, a fall must be allowed for in the surface, to carry off rainwater and avoid puddling along the base of the house wall. If the work is carried out in very hot, dry weather, the stones should be damped before pointing is carried out, or running cracks will very quickly form when the cement has dried.

Concrete paving: Prepare the base as before, using a 4-in. coarse clinker bed. As this surface is solid throughout, an edging is optional. However, shuttering in the form of 6 × 1 in. planks will have to be laid down to form a mould for the concrete until it has set. You may prefer to leave the timber edging in position and the advantage of this is that it prevents garden pests from making their homes in the crevices beneath the concrete.

Prepare a mix, consisting of 3 parts of $\frac{3}{4}$-in. ballast and 1 part of cement, making sure that the aggregate is thoroughly turned over and reduced to an even grey appearance throughout. It is important that no patches of unmixed ballast appear at this stage, as they will undoubtedly cause early cracking and breaking-up of the surface. Let your mix be firm so that it is easily workable on the site.

Set out level marking pegs down the middle of the path and check them carefully for trueness with a spirit level. Now lay down a 3-in. thick bed of concrete, working the mix evenly over the base and hard up against the edging boards. The final level can be produced with a tamping board which you work along the roughly levelled surface bringing the "fat" of the cement along with the board and finishing off flush with the tops of the levelling pegs. At this stage the pegs can either be withdrawn or hammered well below the concrete surface, and their holes filled in with the mix. The surface can be given a running over with a float trowel while it is still moist and this will help to produce a smooth finish.

151

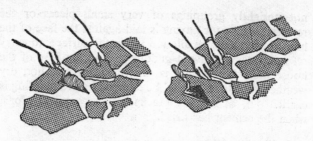

Levels must be constantly checked when laying crazy paving

Crazy paving: A crazy paved path is a most attractive feature if well laid, and has the advantage of being adaptable to an informal and winding pattern. Use either quarried stone such as York, Cotswold, Derbyshire stones, or broken coloured paving stone, which has a warm lively appearance at all times of the year. The base should be prepared in the same way as for the rectangular paved path. The stones on the outside edges should be laid first, following carefully any curves, which you will have already marked out with pegs. Use larger stones on the outside edges, as this makes for greater strength at the weakest points. Levels should be checked with the straightedge and spirit level as each section is laid down. The inside area can now be laid using the straightedge and club hammer to bed down the stones until they are level with the edge stones on each side. Leave a ½-in. gap between the segments of paving for pointing up, and fill the gaps with a 2 and 1 sand/cement mix. Bring the mix flush to the top of the paving, and shape along the edge of each stone with a pointing-trowel so that there is a clean joint and good adherence between the stones.

Make sure that you have good even distribution of colour if you are using precast paving, as the whole effect will be ruined if there are too many uneven blocks of colour over the path surface.

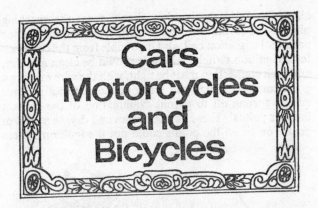

Cars Motorcycles and Bicycles

Locating faults on a car: When a car that normally runs well suddenly "conks out" or refuses to start, the fault is usually minor and not too difficult to remedy – provided you know how to locate it.

The vast majority of breakdowns are due to trouble in either the ignition circuit or the fuel supply system, the former being much more likely. If your engine stops suddenly and without warning, suspicion points immediately to the ignition system. (Though such trouble could also occur, for example, through failure of the timing chain or timing gears, so that the valves and distributor are no longer being driven.) If the engine stops after faltering and losing power for some distance, the trouble may well lie in the fuel system.

The first thing to do is to check that there is petrol in the tank. Don't rely on the fuel gauge; its needle may have stuck. Instead, rock the car and listen at the tank filler for the sound of petrol swilling about. Next, check that there is electrical power available by sounding the horn. If all electrical accessories are dead, check the battery to see whether a lead is loose or detached. A loose battery terminal can often be rectified by giving it a few taps with the heel of a shoe.

Assuming that electric current is available, check over

153

all the leads in the ignition circuit, from the sparking plugs back to the distributor, then from the distributor back to the ignition coil, and if possible from the coil back to the ignition switch. All leads should be clean and dry, and each connection must be tight, with the wire making a good contact. If you can reach it, the distributor cover can be sprung off to permit examination of the contact breaker points. These must be clean and dry, as a spot of grease or oil on the points could put the ignition system

"Provided you know how to locate it!"

out of order completely. Passing a strip of paper gently between the points may be sufficient to clean them.

In some cases, a car's ignition parts are vulnerable to water that gets under the bonnet when driving in heavy rain. The remedy then is to dry off the sparking plugs, distributor and all leads, when normal running should be restored.

It is easy to check whether the ignition system is working if you have a spanner on the car with which a sparking plug can be unscrewed. Detach the lead of any convenient plug, remove the plug, reconnect the lead and lay the plug on a bare metal part of the engine (so that the plug is touching "earth"). Then switch on the ignition and rotate the engine by getting someone to press the starter button or turn the starter handle. If a strong spark can be seen at the points of the plug, all is probably in order.

If the ignition system is working, then the fuel supply becomes suspect. There may be either a mechanical or an electrical pump that draws petrol from the tank and feeds it into the carburettor. Possible troubles here are an obstruction in the pipeline, a faulty pump, or a blockage in one of the fine-bore jets of the carburettor.

Again, a spanner of suitable size will allow a quick test to be made. Undo one end of the pipe that connects the pump with the carburettor – it need only be loosened by a few turns of the union nut. Then rotate the engine as before, remembering to switch on the ignition if an electric pump is fitted. As the pump operates there should be definite spurts of petrol coming through the loose union. If not, there is trouble in the pump or the pipeline, and you will need the assistance of a garage.

A fairly common trouble on the road is breakage and loss of the fan belt. This belt usually drives the fan, the water pump and the dynamo, so losing it means that the engine will quickly become overheated, while the battery will run down because it is not receiving a charging current. The symptoms of fan-belt breakage are over-heating and the red ignition warning light coming on.

It is usually safe to drive on slowly to the next garage, if this is not far away, where a new belt can quickly be fitted. Otherwise, a make-do belt may have to be rigged up, and for this a pair of nylon stockings – begged from a lady passenger! – can be most useful. Slacken the nuts that hold the dynamo and move this machine inwards along its bracket. Then tie the stockings as tightly as possible over the pulleys. Pull back the dynamo to make the stocking belt as tight as possible and retighten the nuts.

If the fan belt has broken and not been noticed, the engine may have overheated sufficiently to cause a seize-up of the working parts. In this case there is nothing to do but allow it to cool right down, then replenish the oil. Start the engine again, and if it seems to be running normally you can risk driving home very carefully. But have the engine examined by a garage as soon as possible in case the seizure has caused damage internally.

If the engine runs normally but the car will not draw away in gear, there is probably trouble in the clutch or, very rarely, the gearbox, and garage assistance will have to be sought.

Punctures: These always happen in the most awkward places and at the worst of times – usually on a dark, wet night, down a country lane in the middle of nowhere. There are, however, ways to make wheel changing a less cumbersome chore.

Make a point of slackening off the wheel nuts before jacking the car up, otherwise the wheel will rotate and make things difficult. If the ground is soft, get a piece of wood, metal, brick or stone, to put underneath the jack. This will even out the weight and prevent it sinking.

The car should not be able to roll while being jacked up, so apply the handbrake if the puncture is in a front wheel; if it is in a rear one, put the car in gear.

When putting on the spare wheel, it may not fit between the hub and the road. The explanation is quite simple; when the weight is taken off the suspension, which is what happens when the car is jacked up, the suspension leg stretches and lowers the hub. The cure is to give the jack a few extra pumps, and you will get enough clearance to fit the wheel. Put the nuts back on, but don't tighten them fully while the wheel is still off the ground – lower the jack and then tighten up. To avoid losing any of the wheel nuts, drop them into the inverted hub cap while working on the car.

A last tip – carry a pair of old gloves and plenty of rags

in the boot of the car to keep your hands and clothes clean.

Breakdowns: Quite often a breakdown occurs which could be overcome if the proper spare part were carried. To make certain that a breakdown could always be dealt with, however, would mean that the car would be like a travelling spare parts shop! As the only essential is to get the car going so that it can be driven to a garage or home, there are many ways to make temporary repairs.

A really common fault is a leaking top hose on the radiator. This spews out water from the cooling system and causes the engine to heat up as well as soaking the electrical and ignition systems. As long as the hose is not too badly damaged, it can be wrapped in rags or polythene bags and bound with adhesive tape or string. This should keep the water in long enough to get to a garage so that a new hose can be bought. Water will still leak but not so badly.

Additional aid can be given to the cooling system by running the car without the radiator filler cap. The cap is pressurized and will tend to increase any leaks; running without it will ease off the pressure, but the car must be driven more slowly than normal until a repair is carried out.

Possibly the most common trouble is caused by the driver who loses his keys and, although he may be able to get into the car, he cannot start it. The number of the key is stamped on the ignition lock so buying a spare key is the obvious answer as long as the shops and garages are open. At night this can be a problem, especially if there are no all-night garages in the district. There is, however, a simple way out.

What has to be done is to connect up the ignition system by by-passing the ignition switch and to do this all that is needed is a length of wire. The wire should be connected from the terminal on the ignition coil marked SW to any live point. The live point can be found in the fuse box by lightly touching each terminal in turn with a piece of wire, with the other end of the wire on the car chassis or body. When a spark is produced it means that the terminal is live (normally the A5 terminal) and the wire can be connected. If the car has a separate ignition switch and starter, pressing the starter button will start the car. In modern cars, with ignition switch and starter combined, it will be necessary to push the solenoid on the starter motor. The "hot" wire must be disconnected at its live end to turn the engine off. If there are only two fuses fitted to the car in the fuse box, a wire or even silver paper, connecting their two live sides, will turn the ignition on.

Silver paper can also be used in place of a fuse that blows or is lost, but do remember to replace it with a proper fuse as soon as possible.

Emergency tools: Women drivers and passengers often carry in their handbags a real treasure trove of odds and ends which can be turned into emergency tools. Nail scissors, nail files and tail combs can be used as tools for all sorts of jobs, while a lipstick can be used to colour an exposed tail bulb if the red lens gets broken. A stick of chewing gum can be chewed until soft and then used to cure a small leak in the petrol tank or round a metal petrol pipe or union near the carburettor.

An elastic band can be used as a return spring on the throttle arm by the carburettor. The proper return spring sometimes breaks, causing the throttle to jam open. This can be frightening and dangerous.

Faults which cannot be cured until the car reaches home such as fast water loss or a slow puncture, where no spare wheel is carried, can be overcome by "garage-hopping". This involves driving into all the garages on the way home and topping up with water or blowing up the offending tyre, enabling another couple of miles to be completed each time.

Starter motors can be difficult at times but there are one or two little tricks you can use to get them going. First, put the car in first gear and then get out and rock it backwards and forwards a few times. If the starter motor has stuck slightly this should free it off. Failing this, there is a nut on the end of the starter motor and a spanner on this will allow it to be turned over and so freed. Starters which won't free with this treatment are, unhappily, damaged and nothing can be done on the spot.

From time to time a car will get sluggish during a run and then refuse to pull away from a standstill. This can be due to binding brakes, which is quite common on older cars. This is caused by rusty parts, but it can be cured by slackening the brake adjustment after the wheels have cooled down. The adjuster is a square nut on the back of the brake drum and this can be turned with a spanner and a click will be heard at each turn. Slacken it off three or four clicks and try the brakes. A real cure cannot be carried out at the roadside so the car should be driven gently, with as little braking as possible until a repair can be done.

Windscreen wipers on British cars get more than their fair share of work and sometimes fail in the middle of a thunderstorm. Try giving the wiper motor a tap or two while the wipers are switched on and if this does not work turn the switch on and off a couple of times.

A length of string can be tied to both wiper arms and then run in a continuous loop through both quarter lights. If there is a passenger in the car, he can work the wipers by pulling the string in alternate directions (the wiper motor should be disconnected from the drive cable first). If the driver is alone, he will have to make do with as many wipes as he gets the chance of during a hold-up in traffic.

The brackets which hold silencers and exhaust pipes to the car rust through very quickly and a loud metallic sound from beneath the car will probably be due to a dragging silencer box or tail pipe. It is no use using string to tie the offending part back as this will burn through almost immediately. Wire is the only thing that will remedy this. A look along the road side or in a lay-by will often produce some (as well as a selection of nuts and bolts if the road is a busy one).

Cleaning the car: The main difference between the dust found inside a home and that on the car is that the latter is harsher and grittier, and contains many more small pieces of stone. That is the reason why water should always be used to get rid of road dust, and the technique is to try to float the dust off the car's surface, so that the water acts as a lubricant. If the dust were merely brushed off it would scratch and damage the car's surface. Detergent will help to dislodge the dirt effectively, but use a proper detergent for car cleaning, and not a household one. Household detergents are too harsh, especially on light-coloured cars. Car shampoos are best for getting rid of dust on a car that is very dirty.

A hose pipe is the most effective method, for then the water really gets under the dirt, smoothing it away so that it does no harm. It is possible to buy a brush to fit on the end of a hose pipe and into which can be fitted soluble pellets of detergent.

On occasions washing alone is not enough to remove the deep grime and oxidation, even if a car shampoo is dissolved in the water. Here a special cleaner has to be used. Cleaners of this kind have an abrasive action, and because of this they should not be employed too often, but they can be used to give the car a good grooming occasionally.

Once the car is clean, it needs a polish to give it that final shine, and to protect it as well. The range of polishes on the market is vast, and it is possible to buy products that give a car longer lasting protection.

Many of the polishes contain a cleaning agent – see the makers' instructions. Even so, an excess of road dust should first of all be washed off with water, before these are applied.

Looking after chrome: The manufacturers put chromium

plating on to a car to give it a luxury finish. Yet in a short time, it seems, the plating has deteriorated, and shabby chrome work gives a car a down-at-heel appearance. In fact, the chrome is one of the most vulnerable parts of a car's exterior and it needs to be well cared for. It should be given a good coating of protective polish – the sort that is used on the bodywork – regularly, especially during winter, when it is really under stress from the elements. Particular attention should be paid to the edges of the chrome, for it is often very thin there.

Chrome work that has rusted and pitted should be treated with one of the special chrome cleaners. Do not use a domestic metal polish, for even the most mildly abrasive metal cleaner can damage the chrome. In very bad cases, the work can be covered with a self-adhesive chromium faced cellulose tape.

Motorcycles should be thoroughly checked at frequent intervals

Mopeds, scooters and motor-cycles: Riders of these vehicles can apply many of the previous checks with a few alterations. As two-wheeled machines rely much more on their rather tiny battery, the fluid level in this must be checked. The distilled water boils away very quickly, especially in hot weather, and must be topped-up regularly to avoid a breakdown.

Motor-cycles and scooters tend to "eat" spark plugs and a spare should always be carried. A non-runner can be transformed by fitting a new plug or cleaning up the existing one.

A baffling fault, which is peculiar to two-strokes, occurs when the rider commits one of two mistakes; first he leaves the petrol tap on when he fills up with his petrol/oil mixture. If the garage attendant puts the oil in first it will run straight down into the carburettor and choke it. The bike will run for a few hundred yards and then come to an abrupt halt. The cure is to turn off the tap and drain the carburettor.

The second mistake is to leave the petrol tap turned on while the engine is stopped in hot weather. The petrol in the mixture will evaporate leaving neat oil, with the same results. To prevent this – turn the tap off.

Bicycles should be properly maintained, giving special attention to tyre pressures

Bicycles: Many more people today are taking to cycling, if only because of the problems of parking a car. New designs in bicycles have increased their popularity, and a good machine will give years of service if properly maintained.

The child who owns a cycle has a marvellous toy, and a convenient means of transport. He also has something that can be used as his first lesson in mechanics. He can be gently led on until he acquires more and more knowledge about it. And at the same time, if he is supervised in giving the machine regular maintenance, he is being helped to make sure the bike he rides will be a safe one.

The first essential for all cycles is proper lubrication, and this should be carried out at regular intervals. Children should be encouraged to undertake this themselves although most youngsters in their enthusiasm pour too much oil into the lubricating points. They should be restrained from this, because an excess of oil does no good whatsoever, and it might get on to clothes – or the brake blocks.

Chain maintenance is important. The chain should be removed, cleaned in a tray of paraffin, and hung up to dry. It should then be soaked in warm graphited oil, and left to drain off again. It can then be wiped dry and replaced.

Make sure that this is done at the correct tension. A tight chain can overstrain both rider and cycle, and a loose one may come off in use. There should be just under an inch of movement in the bottom run of the chain when the top one is tightened by pressing on the pedal with the hand.

The inner cables of the calliper brakes might snap if they are not lubricated. It is a good idea to remove them occasionally, hang them up, make a small funnel with modelling clay or chewing gum, and pour in a small amount of oil. This will then work its way down the whole cable.

Look regularly at the strands of the cable, and when one snaps or unravels buy a new one. It is false economy to attempt to repair a cable, particularly since the cost is so small.

In fact, the whole braking system should be checked regularly, since the blocks wear quite rapidly. Stirrup-type brakes are adjusted on the rods, calliper brakes at the cable ends. Spin the wheels to check that they do not bind.

Buy some new blocks as soon as they are needed, and fit them with the closed ends of the holders facing forwards, otherwise they may fly out in use. Align them properly with the rim of the wheel. The old block can be pushed out with an old screwdriver, but care should be taken to avoid a slip and a nasty cut. The best way is to put the holder in a vice, where the new block can be tapped home with a hammer or mallet.

Truing the wheels when they are badly buckled is a job that cannot be done properly at home, and is best left to a professional. But inspect the wheels, when cleaning the bike, for loose spokes. They will not only throw a wheel out of true, but may also catch in the forks and cause an accident. A loose mudguard is dangerous, too, so check the tightness of the mudguard bolts from time to time.

Also check the head bearings occasionally, by applying the front brake and pushing on the handlebars. Undue play should be taken up, and the steering head checked for free movement. Grasp both pedals and try to move them sideways, and see if the wheels can move sideways when they are held at the rim. If these tests reveal any play, the cycle needs attention from a dealer. Beware of overtightening when working on the bearings, for this may crack the balls or damage the races.

Finally, the machine cannot be ridden safely if the saddle and handlebars are not at the correct height. Adjust these, but check that the nuts are fully tightened, and remember to adjust the brakes if the handlebars have been moved.

Children's Games

Here is a set of indoor games suitable for children's parties.

Spinning the platter: Have the children sit in a circle facing inwards and give each one a number. Start the game yourself by spinning a round bread board on its edge in the centre of the circle and calling out a number. The child with this number then rushes to catch the board before it falls. If the player is successful he then spins the platter and calls a number. If, however, the board falls, a forfeit is demanded.

Contrary shadow: Seat the children in a row, and give two hats to one child. He puts on one of the two hats and gives the other to a child he chooses as his shadow. The shadow then puts on his hat, and from that moment must do the opposite to his partner. When his partner sits, the shadow must stand, and so on, until a mistake is made. Then two other children must act as partners.

Hunt the ring: Thread a small curtain ring through a long length of string then knot the ends to make a circle. The children form a circle taking the string in their hands, except for one who stands in the centre. At the word

165

"Go!" the children quickly run the string through their hands and pass the ring from one to another. The player in the centre must try to discover who has the ring. If he guesses correctly, he then changes place with the player caught with the ring.

Kippers: Cut pieces of paper into fish shapes and give one of them, and a rolled newspaper, to each child. The players then line up at one end of the room, each one placing the "kipper" on the floor in front of him. At the word "Go!" each child uses the newspaper to fan the "kipper" towards the finishing line at the other end of the room. First one home is the winner.

Blind postman: The children sit on a set of chairs in a circle, while one is blindfolded and stands in the middle. The children on the chairs are given the names of towns. When the blindfolded postman calls out the names of two towns the children with these names silently change places, while the postman tries to sit in one of their chairs. When he wins, someone else takes his place.

Apple race: Line the children up in two rows. The first in each rank holds an apple, or similar fruit, under his chin. He has to pass it to the second in the row, who in turn must give it to the third, and so on, with no hands allowed. Should the apple drop, the team must start at the beginning again. The first team to get the apple to the end of the row is the winner.

Musical islands: Scatter pieces of newspaper on the floor – one fewer than the number of children in the game. Make them walk round in a circle until the music stops, when they all have to rush to get on an "island". The one left "swimming" drops out, and the game continues with one fewer "island" each time until just one child is left.

Animal farm: Give each child a piece of paper and pencil, and whisper the name of a different animal in each child's ear. At the word "Go!" they must all make the noise of their own particular animal. When you shout "Stop!", each child must write down the names of the animals he has heard. The one with the most wins.

Noises off: Behind a screen make a series of noises – sharpening a pencil, brushing some clothes, striking a match, drinking some water, eating an apple, etc. The child who guesses most noises right wins the game.

Burst bag relay: The children sit on two rows of chairs facing each other, and they are all given a paper bag. The first in each row runs round the back of the chairs and in front of them to his own seat. When the children sit down again, they must blow up the bag and burst it by hitting it with their hands. At the "pop", the next in the line starts to run, and so on, to see which team can finish first.

Tortoise race: The object of this is not to be first, but to see who comes last. But the children must keep moving all the time. They are "out" if they stop.

O'Grady says: Before the game give each child a few sweets to act as forfeits. Call out a series of commands to the children, but only those prefaced by the remark "O'Grady says" must be obeyed; the others should be ignored. For instance, if you call out "O'Grady says: bark like dogs", then the children should all make barking noises. If you merely say: "Stand on one leg", they should do nothing. Those obeying an incorrect order or ignoring a correct one pay a forfeit. The end of the game can be when only one child is left with forfeits, or when the children have grown tired of it.

Cob-web race: A good end-of-party romp, this, although it needs quite a bit of preparation. Buy a present for every child attending the party, and wrap it up in a box. Fix the end of a long piece of string to each box, and run these lengths of string round the house, tying them round bed and chair legs, the banisters, pinning them to the picture rail and skirting board, getting them all tangled up, but finishing at the same point. At this end fix a label with a number on it. Get the children to draw lots for their number, and let them follow the string to get their prize. They will have enormous fun doing so, especially if you have been very devious in arranging the string, so that they have to keep doubling back on their tracks.

TOYS TO MAKE

Stilts: If necessary the measurements given can be adjusted to suit the height and age of the child for whom the stilts are being made, but a height of 7 ft. with the foot rest 2 ft. from the ground is a good average. The stilts are made of 2-in. sq. softwood, with a foot rest consisting mainly of a 4-in. piece of 3 × 2-in. softwood. Use a 4-in. screw to fix it to the uprights and smear waterproof glue on the meeting edges. Strengthen the joint with an angle bracket underneath. An extra capping piece, shaped as shown opposite from 2 × 1-in. softwood, is added.

Periscope: Buy two handbag mirrors and, from two 16-in. lengths of 2 × ½-in. timber, cut sides of suitable width to fit the mirrors. These are fixed into grooves made from thin pieces of plywood and set at an angle of 45 degrees. The back and front are cut, to a suitable size, from ¼-in. plywood, as are the top and bottom, and the small retaining pieces that hold the mirrors in place.

Bagatelle: A bagatelle board can be made to any convenient size, but that shown in the sketch is a handy size. It is made of ¼-in. plywood, cut to the traditional shape and edged with a strip of ⅛-in. hardboard or plywood. A piece of 1-in. sq. timber fixed underneath 9 in. from the top is used to give the board a tilt. Two fences of ¼-in. plywood are glued and pinned from underneath to form the gulleys for the balls. A length of ½-in. dowel serves as a striker. The scoring rings are formed with brass pins, which must be spaced together closer than the diameter of the balls, which can be marbles or large ball bearings. The scores are: top circle 25; double circle 50 outer, 75 inner; divided circle 70 left, 35 right; small bottom circle 125.

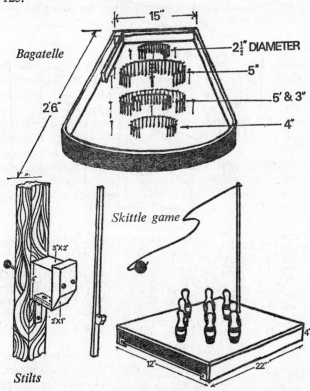

Bagatelle

15"

2½" DIAMETER

5"

5' & 3"

4"

2'6"

Skittle game

Stilts

3"X2"

2"X1"

12"

22"

4"

Skittle game: Skittles are placed on the top of the box, and the idea is to knock them down with a ball on a piece

169

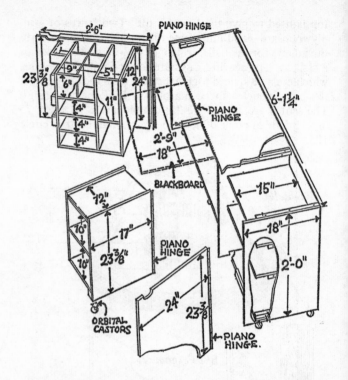

of string fixed to the top of a rod. The skittles can be stored in the base of the box.

The ¼-in. plywood sides (note that one end is shallower) are glued and pinned together, and the plywood bottom is glued and pinned on. An ⅛-in. hardboard lid slides into grooved track, pinned to the sides of the box. The ½-in. rod fits into holes in the lid and box base. Skittles bought from a toy shop are used.

Toy Storage: The play centre shown on the cover of this book was specifically designed to hold large quantities of toys, as well as being an attractive plaything in its own right. It is constructed largely of Handiboard, which is a

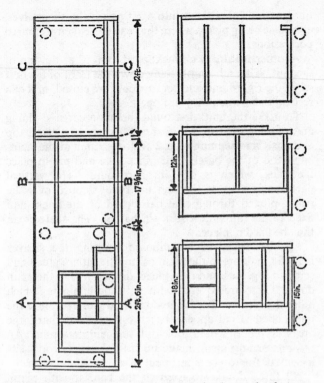

chipboard sold in a series of standard panels that are veneered, not only on both faces but on all edges as well. Where possible, use has been made of standard panels, although a certain amount of cutting has been necessary.

The unit is, in essence, a sideboard mounted on six castors, so that it can be easily moved for cleaning. A vertical partition divides the main carcass into two sections, and shelves are fitted in the right-hand section. An ordinary door is fitted to this section. It is the two doors to the left-hand, larger section that give the play centre its unique qualities, for a whole series of nooks and crannies have been fitted to the back of these, and a child's imagination turns them into exciting toys in themselves, as well as being places where they can store their treasured possessions.

Another feature is a blackboard, hinged at the top of the unit. This can simply hang down the front of the unit when the right-hand and centre doors are closed, or it can rest on them when they are open.

To make the unit, first build the main carcass, gluing and pinning on 1-in. sq. bearers to support shelves, top and base, and pinning on a $2 \times \frac{3}{8}$-in. batten at the right-hand end of the baseboard. Then glue and pin in place the back, which is of $\frac{1}{8}$-in. hardboard. The vertical partition is screwed through the base, stepped over the front, pinned through the hardboard at the back, and fixed to the top with a 1-in. sq. batten. The shelves can then be fixed in place.

All the pieces of Handiboard forming the shelves behind the doors to the main compartment are glued and screwed together, and then glued and screwed to the main door. These are covered with a plastic laminate, which hides the screws. The laminate is used merely to give the unit added visual appeal, because it was felt that large areas of veneer would look dull and uninteresting. An egg-box arrangement, made up from $\frac{3}{8}$-in. plywood, sits loosely in the top compartment of the left-hand door.

All three doors are fixed to the carcass with piano hinges, which are more expensive than ordinary hinges, but are easier for the amateur to fit, because there is no need to chop out notches to receive them. Chipboard does not hold screws as well as natural timber so it is advisable to insert a screw in every hole in the hinge – in timber and other forms of board only every alternate screw-hole needs to be used.

To avoid the expense of handles (which are a potential hazard in a child's room anyway) hand grips are cut in the tops of the doors.

The shelves behind the doors may well carry a considerable weight from time to time, and this will impose a strain on the hinges and the general construction. Because of this, castors are fitted under them. These make their whole operation much more smooth.

The last item to be fitted is the blackboard, which is simply a sheet of Handiboard treated with a special blackboard paint.

The following materials are required to make this unit:

Carcass: Handiboard, one piece 72 × 18 in. (top), one piece 72 × 15 in. (base), two pieces 24 × 18 in. (sides), one piece 24 × 18 in. (cut) (centre division).

Shelves: Handiboard, two pieces 24 × 15 in.

Left-hand door: Handiboard, one piece, 36 × 24 in. (cut) (door front), three pieces 24 × 12 in. (cut) (shelf sides), one piece 36 × 12 in. (cut into three) (shelves). Rest of shelves from offcuts except for two pieces 9 × 6 in. and one piece 12 × 6 in. of ⅜-in. plywood, and four pieces 5 in. sq. of ¼-in. plywood.

Centre door: Handiboard, one piece 24 × 18 in. (cut) (door front).

Shelf side: Handiboard, one piece 24 × 18 in. (cut in two), one piece 18 × 12 in (base).

Right-hand door: Handiboard, one piece 24 in. sq.

Shelves: Handiboard, two pieces 24 × 15 in.

Blackboard: Handiboard, one piece 36 × 18 in. (cut).

Children love to act a play and this simple story, a variation of the traditional Punch and Judy theme, can be performed as a puppet show, or by using favourite toys for the characters, or with children themselves playing the parts.

PUNCH MINDS THE BABY

CHARACTERS
Punch
Judy, his wife
Baby (this is not a proper "character" – it's just a bundle of clothes really)
Joey, the Clown
The Policeman
The Zoo-keeper
Charlie Crocodile

SCENE
The scene is intended to be the inside of Punch and Judy's home, but the only essential piece of "scenery" is a screened-off section to the right of the "stage", meant to

represent a large cupboard. The curtain goes up to show Punch and Judy – Judy is rocking the baby in her arms.

Judy: *Punch! Will you mind the baby while I go out shopping?*

Punch: *Certainly, dear. Certainly, dear. Off you go! Off you go! Off you go!*

Judy: (handing the baby to Punch) *Be sure and take care of him then. If he gets hungry, his bottle of milk is in the cupboard over there. Well, I'm off. . . .* Exit Judy

Punch: *Bye-bye. Bye-bye. Bye-bye . . .* (he looks down at the bundle in his arms). . . . *There, there, then. Shall I sing you to sleep, little baby?*

Baby starts to cry loudly

Punch: *Oh, Shh! Such a noise! I'll sing to you. . . .*
(singing) *Sleep, little baby,*
> *Sleep, little baby,*
> *Pretty little baby,*
> *Pretty little baby,*
> *Sleep – sleep – sleep . . . zzzzzzzzz. . . .*

After a minute, enter Joey the Clown, bounding in exuberantly

Joey: *Hello, hello, hello!* (Stops suddenly when he sees Punch asleep . . .) *Oho – what have we here? Punch and the baby fast asleep. . . . Ha-ha – just the chance for me to play a little trick on him especially as it's April Fool's Day.* (Joey goes up to Punch and very carefully takes the baby from him so as not to waken him) *Carefully does it . . . mustn't waken him. Now, little baby, into the cupboard with you for a while. Won't Punch get a fright when he wakes up and finds you gone.* (He pulls the curtain back from "cupboard" and puts Baby inside, replacing the curtain again) *Now to waken Punch. . . .* (Joey goes off stage for a minute, reappears with large blown-up paper bag. He goes up behind the sleeping Punch, and bangs it loudly. Punch wakens up with a start, Joey disappears quickly . . .)

Punch: *Help! Help! Help!... What was that?* ... (he
rushes from side to side across the stage ...) *Oh dear,
I must have dropped off for a minute. Now where was
I?* ... (suddenly realizes Baby is missing) *Oh –
Baby.... Where is he? Where is he? Where is he?...*
Enter Judy, with shopping bag

Judy: *What on earth is the matter with you, Punch, running
round in circles like that? Stop at once!*

Punch: *Oh dear, oh dear, oh dear!*

Judy: (suspiciously) *Punch – where's Baby?*

Punch: *Well – I think he's gone for a walk ... or a swim
maybe ...*

Judy: (advancing in anger on Punch) *A walk? A swim?
Don't be silly – babies can't walk or swim.... Punch –
have you lost him? ... What have you done to him?*

Punch: (regaining control) *I've not done anything, you silly
Judy, so stop getting so cross. Take that!* (hits her on
head with stick – she falls down) *Silly thing. That'll
keep her quiet for a bit. She can go in the cupboard till
I find Baby, then I'll waken her up.* (He pulls back
curtain, pushes Judy inside cupboard)
Enter Policeman

Punch: *Aha, just the man I wanted...* (knocks Policeman's
helmet off with his stick) *I've lost Baby – have you got
him? Thought he might be under there....*

Policeman: (putting helmet back) *No, I have not got
him.... I heard noises – thought I'd better investigate.
Now* (getting out notebook) *when did you last see Baby?*

Punch: *Five minutes ago. I was singing to him ... like this*
(starts singing again) *Sleep, little baby,*
     Sleep, little baby,
     Pretty little baby.... zzzzz....
(within seconds, both Punch and the Policeman have
dozed off, and are snoring away)
Enter agitated Zoo-keeper

Zoo-keeper: *Oh dear, what shall I do? What shall I do?
I must find a policeman. ... Aha, here he is – fast
asleep. I say, waken up, Mr. Policeman, waken up ...*

there's a good chap. (He pokes Policeman and Punch awake both of whom immediately hit the Zoo-keeper over the head, Punch with his stick, Policeman with his truncheon, because they get such a fright . . .)

Policeman: *Now then, Zoo-keeper, I'll take your name and address if you're not careful. . . .*

Zoo-keeper: *Oh, you've got my name and address already – don't make such a fuss. You must help me, Policeman – I've lost Charlie Crocodile from the Zoo. He's just clean disappeared and I don't know where to look . . .*

Policeman: *Dear me! First a missing baby – now a missing crocodile . . . you can't expect me to find everything, you know . . . The Lost Property office is already full of gloves and umbrellas. . . .*

Punch: (knocking Policeman's helmet off again . . .) *Now you see what you've done – I bet Charlie Crocodile has taken Baby, and eaten him for supper by now too . . .*

Zoo-keeper: *Oh, no, no, no! I'm sure Charlie would never do such a thing. . . .*

Punch: *Well, we'll see. Come on – we'll all go and hunt for Charlie*

Punch and Zoo-keeper exeunt, Zoo-keeper first, being poked in the back by Punch's stick. Policeman left alone on stage . . .

Policeman: *Hmmm! To tell you the truth, I'm not very fond of crocodiles myself . . . In fact, I'm really just a bit frightened – I think I'll hide somewhere till they've found Charlie . . . Aha, I'll hide in Punch's cupboard.*

So Policeman pulls back curtain and goes into cupboard. Charlie Crocodile suddenly appears, dances across stage and out the other side

Enter Zoo-keeper and Punch

Punch: *I just don't know where to look!* (Appeals to audience) *Have you seen Charlie anywhere?* (Audience presumably will reply "Yes" and point to direction Charlie went out)

Zoo-keeper: *Oh quick – he went that way. . . .*

Exeunt Zoo-keeper and Punch by the way that

177

Charlie left. But as they go off, in comes Charlie and dances across and out the other side. Zoo-keeper and Punch re-enter

Punch: *Well we can't find him* . . . *Are you sure he went that way?* (Audience again, presumably, will point to other direction)

Zoo-keeper: *Quick – this way, Punch* . . .

Exeunt Punch and Zoo-keeper in other direction. Again Charlie reappears and dances across and out opposite side. Zoo-keeper and Punch come back

Punch: (hitting Zoo-keeper over the head lightly) *Stupid Zoo-keeper. Where is Charlie?*

Zoo-keeper: *I'll tell you what we'll do – Charlie loves a nice juicy piece of steak* . . . *we'll lure Charlie back with that* . . . (While they are talking, Charlie comes back in and stays just behind the two of them. Presumably audience will shout out at this point, but Punch and Zoo-keeper cannot understand what all the fuss is about, and don't realize that Charlie is standing right behind them, watching with great interest)

Zoo-keeper: (producing piece of steak from pocket) *Now here's a lovely juicy piece of steak.*

Punch: *Let's lay it down right here.* . . . (but before he can do anything with it Charlie comes forward and takes steak out of Zoo-keeper's hands . . .)

Punch: (frightened on seeing Charlie) *Help! Help! Help!*

Zoo-keeper: (joyfully hugging Charlie) *Oh Charlie – I knew you'd come back – you were naughty to run away. . .*

Punch: (realizing Charlie is quite friendly, stops being frightened and hits Charlie over the head – has no effect on him at all, being a thick-skinned crocodile) *What have you done with Baby, Charlie? Have you eaten him?*

Charlie: (very upset) *Eaten Baby? Certainly not – I'd never do such a dreadful thing* . . . *what an awful – awwf-ffuuuulll* . . . *boo-hoo-boo-hooo.* . . . (Charlie dissolves in tears)

Zoo-keeper: *There now, see what you've done! Charlie is*

very tenderhearted and you've made him cry by suggesting such a dreadful thing ... There, there, Charlie, don't cry. You go and find Policeman, Punch, while I cheer Charlie up.

Punch: *Huh! Stupid!* (goes off very angry)

Zoo-keeper: (still comforting Charlie) *Don't cry, Charlie. It's all right now....*

Charlie: *I feel – so-so-so t-t-t-tired – sob – after d-d-d-dancing about so much. I'd like to have a r-r-r-rest ...*

Zoo-keeper: *Of course, Charlie. Look, there's a nice cupboard over there. Why don't you go in there for forty winks and I'll wake you up when Punch gets back.* (So Zoo-keeper pulls back curtain and pushes Charlie inside cupboard)

Enter Punch

Punch: *Can't see Policeman anywhere ... we'll have to report him to the Lost Property office now*

Zoo-keeper: *I've an idea, Punch – if the steak lured Charlie back, why don't you lure Baby back with his bottle of milk?*

Punch: *What a splendid idea, Zoo-keeper. I'll do that. The bottle is over in the cupboard – I'll get it now ...* Punch goes over to cupboard and this time pulls curtain all the way back. Inside is Charlie happily lying down, and sitting on his back are Policeman, Judy, leaning against him, and Baby in her arms ... They are all asleep ...

Punch: *Well, bless my soul! Bless my soul! Bless my soul! Here is everyone safe and sound. ...*

Enter Joey the Clown with another blown-up paper bag. Bangs it and everyone wakes up with a jump

Joey: *Ha ha! April Fool, Punch!*

Punch: *Ho! April Fool, yourself.* (Hits him over the head, but Joey doesn't mind) *Let's play ring-a-ring o' roses to celebrate. Hooray!*

Everyone, including Charlie starts a wild dance and song.

CURTAIN

Some Useful Addresses

Association of British Launderers and Cleaners, 16, Lancaster Gate, London, W.2

Association of British Travel Agents, 50, Charlotte Street, London, W.1

Association of Certified and Corporate Accountants, 22, Bedford Square, London, W.C.1

Association of R.A.C. Registered Motor Schools and Driving Instructors, 83/85, Pall Mall, London, S.W.1

Automobile Association, Fanum House, Leicester Square, London, W.C.2

British Aluminium Company Ltd., Norfolk House, St. James's Square, London, S.W.1

British Antique Dealers Association Ltd., 20, Rutland Gate, London, S.W.7

British Carpet Centre, Dorland House, 14/16, Lower Regent Street, London, S.W.1

British Ceramic Tile Council, Federation House, Stoke-on-Trent, Staffs.

British Council for the Rehabilitation of the Disabled, Tavistock House South, Tavistock Square, London, W.C.1

British Cycle and Motor Cycle Industries Association, Starley House, Eaton Road, Coventry.

British Cycling Bureau, Greater London House, Hampstead Road, London, N.W.1

British Electrical Development Association, Inc., 1, Charing Cross, London, S.W.1

British Footwear Manufacturers' Federation, Royalty House, 72, Dean Street, London, W.1

British Furniture Manufacturers' Federated Associations, 17, Berners Street, London, W.1

British Legion, 49, Pall Mall, London, S.W.1

British Lighting Council, Ltd., Brettenham House, 16/18, Lancaster Place, London, W.C.2

British Limbless Ex-Servicemen's Association, 105, Cannon Street, London, E.C.4

British Medical Association, Tavistock Square, London, W.C.1

British Red Cross Society, 14, Grosvenor Crescent, London, S.W.1

British Safety Council, Mason House, 163, Praed Street, London, W.2

British Standards Institution, 2, Park Street, London, W.1

British Woodwork Manufacturers' Association, Sackville House, 40, Piccadilly, London, W.1

Building Centre, 26, Store Street, London, W.C.1

Building Research Station, Bucknalls Lane, Garston, near Watford, Herts.

Building Societies Association, 14, Park Street, London, W.1

Butter Information Council, Salisbury House, London Wall, London, E.C.2

Camping Club of Great Britain and Ireland Ltd., 11, Lower Grosvenor Place, London, S.W.1

Cement and Concrete Association, 52, Grosvenor Gardens, London, S.W.1

Central Council of Physical Recreation, 26, Park Crescent, London, W.1

Chartered Auctioneers' and Estate Agents' Institute, 29, Lincoln's Inn Fields, London, W.C.2

Cheese Bureau, The, 40, Berkeley Square, London, W.1

Christian Aid, 10, Eaton Gate, London, S.W.1

Church Army, 185, Marylebone Road, London, N.W.1

Coal Utilization Council, 19, Rochester Row, London, S.W.1

Consumer Council, 3, Cornwall Terrace, London, N.W.1

Consumers Association, 14, Buckingham Street, London, W.C.2

Copper Development Association, 55, South Audley Street, London, W.1

Council for Nature, Zoological Gardens, Regent's Park, London, N.W.1

Design Centre, 28, Haymarket, London, S.W.1

Provincial Centres:
Bristol Building and Design Centre, Stonebridge House, Colston Avenue, The Centre, Bristol, 1

Midland Design and Building Centre, Mansfield Street, Nottingham.

Manchester Building and Design Centre, 115, Portland Street, Manchester, 1

Engineering and Building Centre, Broad Street, Birmingham.

Electrical Association for Women, 25, Foubert's Place, London, W.1

Electrical Development Association, Trafalgar Buildings, 1, Charing Cross, London, S.W.1

Esso Heating Advisory Service, 16, Charles II Street, Haymarket, London, S.W.1

Fairy Snow Facts Service, 47, Reeves Mews, London, W.1

Federation of British Rubber and Allied Manufacturers, Trafalgar House, 9, Whitehall, London, S.W.1

Fibre Building Board Development Organization Ltd., Buckingham House, 6, Buckingham Street, London, W.C.2

Fire Protection Association, Aldermary House, Queen Street, London, E.C.4

Fisons Horticulture Ltd., P.O. Box 2, Harvest House, Princes Street, Ipswich, Suffolk.

Flowers Publicity Council Ltd., Agriculture House, Knightsbridge, London, S.W.1

Food Information Centre, 36, Park Street, Croydon, Surrey.

Gas Council, 4/5, Grosvenor Place, London, S.W.1

Gypsum Plasterboard Development Association, P.O. Box 321, London, N.W.1

Heating and Ventilating Contractors' Association, Coastal Chambers, 172, Buckingham Palace Road, London, S.W.1

Heating Centre, 34, Mortimer Street, London, W.1

Her Majesty's Stationery Office, Atlantic House, Holborn Viaduct, London, E.C.1

Incorporated Association of Architects and Surveyors, 29, Belgrave Square, London, S.W.1

Law Society, The, 113, Chancery Lane, London, W.C.2

Leather Institute, Leather Trade House, 9, St. Thomas Street, London, S.E.1

Linoleum Manufacturers' Association, Vernon House, Sicilian Avenue, Bloomsbury Square, London, W.C.1

London Federation of Boys' Clubs, 22, Blackfriars Road, London, S.E.1

Lux Washability Bureau, 21/23, New Fetter Lane, London, E.C.4

Milk Marketing Board, Thames Ditton, Surrey.

National Anti-Vivisection Society, 51, Harley Street, London, W.1

National Bedding Federation, 157, Victoria Street, London, S.W.1

National Canine Defence League, 10, Seymour Street, London, W.1

National Caravan Council, Ltd., 40, Piccadilly, London, W.1

National Coal Board, Hobart House, Grosvenor Place, London, S.W.1

National Corporation for the Care of Old People, Nuffield Lodge, Regent's Park, London, N.1

National Dairy Council, 145, Charing Cross Road, London, W.C.2

National Federation of Dyers and Cleaners, Glen House, Stag Place, London, S.W.1

National Federation of Women's Institutes, 39, Eccleston Street, London, S.W.1

National House Builders Registration Council, 58, Portland Place, London, W.1

National Marriage Guidance Council, 58, Queen Anne Street, London, W.1

National Old People's Welfare Council, 26, Bedford Square, London, W.C.1

National Playing Fields Association, 57b, Catherine Place, London, S.W.1

National Research Development Corporation, P.O. Box 236, Kingsgate House, 66/74 Victoria Street, London, S.W.1

National Society for Mentally Handicapped Children, 5, Bulstrode Street, London, W.1

National Society for the Prevention of Cruelty to Children, 1, Riding House Street, London, W.1

National Spastics Society, 12, Park Crescent, London, W.1

National Trust, 42, Queen Anne's Gate, London, S.W.1

Noise Abatement Society, 6, Old Bond Street, London, W.1

Oxfam, 274, Banbury Road, Oxford.

Pedestrians Association for Road Safety, 4, College Hill, London, E.C.4

Persil Home Washing Bureau, 21, New Fetter Lane, London, E.C.4

Regent Oil Co., Ltd., 117, Park Street, London, W.1

Rentokil Laboratories Ltd., 16, Dover Street, London, W.1

Road Haulage Association, 22, Upper Woburn Place, London, W.C.1

Royal Automobile Club, 83/85, Pall Mall, London, S.W.1

Royal College of Nursing and National Council of Nurses of the United Kingdom, 1a, Henrietta Place, London, W.1

Royal Horticultural Society, Wisley, Ripley, Woking, Surrey.

Royal Institute of British Architects, 66, Portland Place, London, W.1

Royal National Institute for the Blind, 224, Great Portland Street, London, W.1

Royal National Institute for the Deaf, 105, Gower Street, London, W.C.1

Royal Society for the Prevention of Accidents, 52, Grosvenor Gardens, London, S.W.1

Royal Society for the Prevention of Cruelty to Animals, 105, Jermyn Street, London, S.W.1

Royal Yachting Association, 171, Victoria Street, London, S.W.1

Salvation Army, 101, Queen Victoria Street, London, E.C.4

Save the Children Fund, 29, Queen Anne's Gate, London, S.W.1

Shell-Mex and B.P. Group, Domestic Fuels Division, Shell-Mex House, Strand, London, W.C.2

Ship and Boat Builders National Federation, 31, Great Queen Street, London, W.C.2

Society of Chiropodists, 8, Wimpole Street, London, W.1

Solid Smokeless Fuels Federation, York House, Empire Way, Wembley, Middlesex.

Spastics Society, 12, Park Crescent, London, W.1

Timber Research and Development Association Ltd., The Building Centre, 26, Store Street, London, W.C.1

Vitreous Enamel Development Council Ltd., 28, Welbeck Street, London, W.1

Women's Advisory Council on Solid Fuel, 18, South Molton Street, London, W.1

Women's Gas Federation, 5, Grosvenor Crescent, London, S.W.1

Women's Home Industries Ltd., 6, Douglas Street, London, S.W.1

Women's Royal Voluntary Service, 17, Old Park Lane, London, W.1

Youth Hostels Association, Trevelyan House, St. Albans, Herts.

Youth Hostels Association of Northern Ireland Ltd., (1931), 28, Bedford Street, Belfast.

Youth Hostels Association (Scottish) (1931), 7, Bruntsfield Crescent, Edinburgh, 10

INDEX

189

190